TAKING YOUR PLACE AT THE TOP

ALSO FROM REVIVAL TODAY

Financial Overflow

Dominion Over Sickness and Disease

Boldly I Come

Twenty Secrets for an Unbreakable Marriage

How to Dominate in a Wicked Nation

Seven Wrong Relationships

Everything a Man Should Be

Understanding the World in Light of Bible Prophecy

Are You Going Through a Crisis?

The 20 Laws that Govern the Financial Anointing

35 Questions for Those Who Hate the Prosperity Gospel

The Art of Spiritual Warfare

Help for Your Darkest Time

Seven Reasons Your Church Will Never Have Revival

Who Told You You're in a Season of Waiting?

How to Prevail in Every Battle of Life

Decisions Determine Destiny

Twenty-Four Changes to Immediately Improve Your Happiness

Taking Your Place at the Top

The Path to Dominion: A 16-Week Devotional to Walk in God's Plan for Your Life

TAKING YOUR PLACE AT THE TOP

52 SECRETS OF UNCOMMON ACHIEVERS

JONATHAN SHUTTLESWORTH

with
ADALIS SHUTTLESWORTH

Without limiting the rights under copyright(s) reserved below, no part of this publication may be reproduced, stored in, or introduced into a retrieval system or transmitted in any form or by any means (electronic, mechanical, photocopying, recording, or otherwise) without the prior permission of the publisher and the copyright owner.

The content of this book is provided "AS IS." The publisher and the author make no guarantees or warranties as to the accuracy, adequacy, or completeness of or results to be obtained from using the content of this book, including any information that can be accessed through hyperlinks or otherwise, and expressly disclaim any warranty expressed or implied, including but not limited to implied warranties of merchantability or fitness for a particular purpose. This limitation of liability shall apply to any claim or cause whatsoever, whether such claim or cause arises in contract, tort, or otherwise. In short, you, the reader, are responsible for your choices and the results they bring.

The scanning, uploading, and distributing of this book via the internet or any other means without the permission of the publisher and copyright owner is illegal and punishable by law. Please purchase only authorized copies, and do not participate in or encourage piracy of copyrighted materials. Your support of the author's rights is appreciated.

Unless otherwise indicated, Scripture references are taken from the HOLY BIBLE, NEW LIVING TRANSLATION (NLT), Copyright© 1996, 2004, 2007 by Tyndale House Foundation. Used by permission of Tyndale House Publishers, Inc., Carol Stream, Illinois 60188. All rights reserved. Used by permission.

Scriptures marked KJV are taken from the KING JAMES VERSION (KJV), public domain.

Scriptures marked TLB are taken from THE LIVING BIBLE copyright© 1971. Used by permission of Tyndale House Publishers, Inc., Carol Stream, Illinois 60188. All rights reserved.

Scriptures marked NKJV are taken from the NEW KING JAMES VERSION®. Copyright© 1982 by Thomas Nelson, Inc. Used by permission. All rights reserved.

Scriptures marked AMPC are taken from the AMPLIFIED® BIBLE (AMPC), Copyright © 1954, 1958, 1962, 1964, 1965, 1987 by the Lockman Foundation. Used by Permission. (www.Lockman.org)

Scriptures marked ESV are taken from THE HOLY BIBLE, ENGLISH STANDARD VERSION ® Copyright© 2001 by Crossway, a publishing ministry of Good News Publishers. Used by permission.

Scripture text within the body, shown in italics, is from multiple unspecified translations or the author's paraphrase.

Copyright © 2026 by Revival Today. All rights reserved.

Released March 2026

ISBN: 978-1-64457-658-8 (Pb)
ISBN: 978-1-64457-659-5 (Hc)

Rise UP Publications
www.riseUPpublications.com
Phone: 866-846-5123

CONTENTS

Introduction   11

1. Secret 1   17
   Uncommon Achievers Reject Failure
2. Secret 2   23
   Uncommon Achievers Establish a Clear-Cut Goal
3. Secret 3   27
   Uncommon Achievers Receive God's Stamp of Approval
4. Secret 4   29
   Uncommon Achievers Announce Their Goal and Explain Its Value and Purpose
5. Secret 5   31
   Uncommon Achievers Value the Greatness of Their Goals and Are Proud of Them
6. Secret 6   35
   Uncommon Achievers Develop a Detailed Plan
7. Secret 7   37
   Uncommon Achievers Acknowledge Their Limitations
8. Secret 8   39
   Uncommon Achievers Establish a Reputation of Integrity
9. Secret 9   43
   Uncommon Achievers Consult Other Achievers
10. Secret 10   47
    Uncommon Achievers Establish a First-Class Quality Standard
11. Secret 11   53
    Uncommon Achievers Acknowledge Those Who Help Them
12. Secret 12   57
    Uncommon Achievers Involve as Many People as Possible in Their Endeavors
13. Secret 13   61
    Uncommon Achievers Organize and Delegate Responsibilities
14. Secret 14   63
    Uncommon Achievers Use the Expertise of Specialists

15. Secret 15   65
Uncommon Achievers Make Contract Details and Expectations Very Clear

16. Secret 16   67
Uncommon Achievers Compensate and Reward Those Who Assist Them in Achieving Their Goals

17. Secret 17   75
Uncommon Achievers Keep the Enthusiasm and Greatness of Their Project Alive

18. Secret 18   79
Uncommon Achievers Only Hire Happy People

19. Secret 19   85
Uncommon Achievers Establish a Schedule for Their Goals and Begin Working

20. Secret 20   87
Uncommon Achievers Establish Order and Flow in Everything They Do

21. Secret 21   91
Uncommon Achievers Are Lifetime Students

22. Secret 22   97
Uncommon Achievers Honor the Law of Sight

23. Secret 23   103
Uncommon Achievers Admit When They Are Wrong

24. Secret 24   107
Uncommon Achievers Remain Humble by Honoring God and His Church

25. Secret 25   115
Uncommon Achievers Understand Their Business Is a God-Given Means to Create Wealth

26. Secret 26   123
Uncommon Achievers Navigate Forward While in Crisis

27. Secret 27   125
Uncommon Achievers Don't Allow Others' Crises to Determine Their Actions

28. Secret 28   129
Uncommon Achievers Are Immune to the Opinions of Others

29. Secret 29   135
Uncommon Achievers Refuse to Have Grasshopper Complex

30. Secret 30   141
Uncommon Achievers Have Ethics and Follow the Law

31. Secret 31   145
Uncommon Achievers Accept the Life of a Rich Man and the Persecution That Comes With It

32. Secret 32   149
Uncommon Achievers Move Quickly

33. Secret 33   155
Uncommon Achievers Are Excellent

34. Secret 34   159
Uncommon Achievers Embrace Their Unique Skill Set and Rare Talent Stack

35. Secret 35   163
Uncommon Achievers Run Hard

36. Secret 36   165
Uncommon Achievers Confront Sin

37. Secret 37   169
Uncommon Achievers Think About Ways to Generate Money, Not Ways to Save Money

38. Secret 38   173
Uncommon Achievers Do Things That Have Never Been Done Before

39. Secret 39   177
Uncommon Achievers Value Time

40. Secret 40   181
Uncommon Achievers Hire the Best of the Best

41. Secret 41   185
Uncommon Achievers Don't Tolerate Disloyalty

42. Secret 42   193
Uncommon Achievers Honor the Law of Admiration

43. Secret 43   199
Uncommon Achievers Do Not Assume the Best of Everyone in the Area of Finances

44. Secret 44   203
Uncommon Achievers Don't Assume the Best of People or Their Motives

45. Secret 45   207
Uncommon Achievers Know What They're Called to Do and Recognize What They're Not Called to Do

46. Secret 46   211
Uncommon Achievers Are Generous People

47. Secret 47   215
Uncommon Achievers Can Work with Those They Don't Fully Agree with

48. Secret 48   219
Uncommon Achievers Are Not Entitled People

49. Secret 49   221
Uncommon Achievers Understand They Will Lose What They Don't Protect

50. Secret 50   225
Uncommon Achievers Notice Trends—They Don't Wait for Crises

51. Secret 51   229
Uncommon Achievers Think Generationally

52. Secret 52   231
Uncommon Achievers Can Gain the Whole World without Losing Their Soul

Afterword   235
Notes   239
Jonathan and Adalis Shuttlesworth   241

INTRODUCTION

Uncommon achievement isn't your ambition—it's your birthright. You don't have to strive for success and prosperity. God conferred prosperity and success upon you through redemption. In the same way a curse belongs to those outside of God, prosperity and success belong to those who abide in God. You don't have to strive to attain something you don't have—you can simply walk in what's yours.

> "Moses my servant is dead. Therefore, the time has come for you to lead these people, the Israelites, across the Jordan River into the land I am giving them. I promise you what I promised Moses: 'Wherever you set foot, you will be on land I have given you— from the Negev wilderness in the south to the Lebanon mountains in the north, from the Euphrates River in the east to the Mediterranean

INTRODUCTION

Sea in the west, including all the land of the Hittites.' No one will be able to stand against you as long as you live. For I will be with you as I was with Moses. I will not fail you or abandon you. Be strong and courageous, for you are the one who will lead these people to possess all the land I swore to their ancestors I would give them. Be strong and very courageous. Be careful to obey all the instructions Moses gave you. Do not deviate from them, turning either to the right or to the left. **Then you will be successful in everything you do.** Study this Book of Instruction continually. Meditate on it day and night so you will be sure to obey everything written in it. **Only then will you prosper and succeed in all you do.** This is my command—be strong and courageous! Do not be afraid or discouraged. For the Lord your God is with you wherever you go."

— JOSHUA 1:2-9 (NLT)

"If you fully obey the Lord your God and carefully keep all his commands that I am giving you today, the Lord your God will set you high above all the nations of the world."

— DEUTERONOMY 28:1

 God has a place at the top for you.

INTRODUCTION

Your obedience to God will secure you a place at the top, and the top is where you belong. Many people aren't interested in what God has for them, and they disguise their disinterest in many different ways, but you don't arrive at the top without intent. Salvation alone won't secure you a place at the top. Living a good life won't do it either. We all know good Christian people who struggle in life.

> So God created human beings in his image. In the image of God he created them; male and female he created them. Then God blessed them and said, **"Be fruitful and multiply."**
>
> — GENESIS 1:27-28

You'll never go somewhere you think you don't belong. If you believe you can't afford to eat at a certain restaurant, you'll never eat there. If you think a private club is too expensive, you'll never end up inside. These seem like carnal things spiritual people should not be concerned about, but the desire within you to reach for more is not carnal—it's something God placed in you. If you don't know and accept that fact, you'll fight against it. You'll listen to people who take Scripture out of context and say, "Well, the Bible says to be content with what we have." The Bible doesn't contradict itself. Scriptures about contentment don't undermine God's first instruction to man in Genesis 1:28, *"Be fruitful and multiply."*

I'm very thankful for everything God has given me, both personally and in ministry. I'm not discontent. I'm as relaxed

INTRODUCTION

as can be, but I'm not content to stay still. I'm reaching for more. I'm always looking to double what God has done within the next four or five weeks. We always have plans in place to multiply what's been given to us. Shrinking back from what God has called you to do to bask in His presence is not the height of spirituality. Being in God's presence will compel you to multiply and bear fruit for the Master. The first command God gave man was not, "Don't commit adultery;" it was, "Be fruitful and multiply."

The desire to reach for more is not a fleshly impulse you need to crush and gain victory over—it's an innate longing that God has put in you. The Bible says God has *"planted eternity in the human heart"* (Ecclesiastes 3:11). Eternity is a boundless existence filled with endless possibilities that God has granted us access to by placing it directly in our hearts. As believers, we have eternal life through our salvation. Eternal life and the benefits that come with it are not just meant to be experienced after we die but lived to the fullest while we're here on Earth (John 10:10). God has designed us to pursue and seize these limitless possibilities, not only in eternity but also here on Earth. Yet, the endless potential of who we can be and what we can achieve can only be accomplished through our personal walk with Christ and obedience to the instructions in His Word.

You must understand that there are two parts to Jesus: the person of Jesus and the principles of Jesus. The person of Jesus gets you to Heaven. You serve, love, and receive Him. The principles of Jesus cause you to be successful on the

INTRODUCTION

Earth. The same is true of the Bible. The power of the Gospel heals your body and transforms your mind, but the principles of the Bible guarantee your success in life. Many people focus on one part of Jesus or the other. Some ministers know about the power of God, and they perform notable miracles, but they don't have enough money to get their car fixed, or their marriage is a mess. Then, other ministers prefer to turn the Bible into a workbook of success principles and never see anyone healed or any manifestation of the power of God in their services in one hundred years of Sundays.

One major purpose of the Bible is to give you instruction for good success in life, ministry, business, marriage, and raising children. When you follow the instructions contained in the Bible, frustration is eliminated. The Bible is a book of instruction and not simply a book of promises or a history text that records the lives of people who lived thousands of years ago. The Bible highlights the lives of uncommon achievers like Christ, David, Solomon, the Apostle Paul, and the list goes on. As you examine the lives of these men and analyze their choices, you discover the uncommon actions they took, which produced their uncommon lives. Since God is no respecter of persons (Romans 2:11), the steps men and women in the Bible took are repeatable. If you do what they did with the same heart they had, you'll get what they took hold of. When you put God's Kingdom first out of love for Him, as Solomon acted out of affection for the Temple of the Lord, you'll reap the same blessings. When you let God's power transform your heart and mind, it produces the same motivation and intention that led these uncommon achievers to take their steps and receive the blessing of God in their lives.

This book outlines 52 secrets that will help you take your place at the top.

SECRET 1

UNCOMMON ACHIEVERS REJECT FAILURE

> Be careful to obey all the instructions Moses gave you. Do not deviate from them, turning either to the right or to the left. Then you will be successful in everything you do.
>
> — JOSHUA 1:7

I value success. You will never attain what you do not value. I see no value in failure.

I recently listened to a song with lyrics that discussed learning from pain. However, I don't see any benefit in pain or failure. God didn't promise to teach you through failure and pain when you follow Him. There's nothing He wants you to know that can't be learned from His Word. Failure doesn't belong to me. I reject failure.

Before I ever started a church, I knew it would never be a small, struggling church. I had no plans to struggle as an evangelist or as a pastor. If you own a business, plan for it to be the best business of its kind. There's always a day of small beginnings, but refuse to stay small. If you're not doing the right things, working harder won't produce a successful outcome. If you put sugar in your gas tank, you wouldn't expect it to start working because you continued to fill it with sugar. Many people are doing it wrong, and if they continue doing it the wrong way, success will never come.

> Study this Book of Instruction continually. Meditate on it day and night so you will be sure to obey everything written in it. Only then will you prosper and succeed in all you do.
>
> — JOSHUA 1:8

I once posted Joshua 1:8 on social media without commentary, and the reaction I received from Christians should surprise you. Ministers and Bible college students replied by saying things like, "God doesn't call us to be successful; He calls us to be faithful." Why would ministers, and people training for ministry take shots at success when faithfulness to the Word guarantees success?

 If you obey God's instructions, you will have prosperity and success.

I don't have a soft spot for failure. I don't abide by little sayings that make me feel good in case I fail. There is no place in the Bible where Jesus failed. Don't tell me Jesus was a failure, and don't tell me His Word makes me a failure. Jesus started with one hundred and twenty people in the upper room. Then, The Church grew to three thousand, then five thousand, then all of Jerusalem, and now there are over 2 billion Christians all over the world. His Word brings prosperity and success. Let's be clear: there's no success without prosperity. Don't ascribe to some religious idea of success.

 There is no success without prosperity.

Financial prosperity alone does not make you successful, but there is no success without it. Prosperity won't necessarily birth success in life, but success will birth prosperity. There are countless stories of people who won the lottery and ended up broke. It usually ruins their life—they achieve nothing, and the financial prosperity destroys them. It is impossible to have success in what God has called you to do without it producing prosperity.

Our church continues to experience rapid multiplication. While it was still in its first year, the server at a nearby restaurant asked me if I knew the building next door was a church that was packed every Sunday. He told me people fly in from all over the world to visit. He had no idea he was speaking to the pastor of the church he was raving about. Your success doesn't just bring prosperity to you—it brings prosperity to your surroundings. If your church grew to five thousand people, there would be five thousand people looking for a place to eat after every church service.

When Bishop T.D. Jakes was hosting Manpower events, the City of Atlanta gave him a massive venue to use that could seat up to 70,000 people. They gave him the venue for free because so many people came to the city and spent so much money at restaurants and hotels that they wanted him there.

Don't adopt a lame religious cliche about success that claims you can be successful even if no one on Earth ever knows your name because God knows it in Heaven. God knows the Devil's name too. There's no way to accomplish the fullness of what God has called you to do if no one knows your name. Part of the Abrahamic blessing is that God will *bless you and make your name great* (Genesis 12:2). That's what God told Abraham, and everything God promised Abraham belongs to us (Galatians 3:29).

> **God will bless you and make your name great.**

For those who make dumb remarks like, "I don't want to be famous. I just want to make Your name famous," I want to clue you in on two things: first, Jesus' name is already famous. Second, if you seek to make His name famous often enough, it will result in your name becoming famous. No one would argue that Billy Graham ever set out to make his name famous, but he became the second most recognized man in the world, behind Muhammad Ali.

When I refer to success, I'm describing the type of success where people know you have success. Rex Humbard was an Ohio pastor who, at one time, had the largest church in the United States. Executives from Fortune 500 corporations would fly to his church or fly him to their business to ask him questions. They wanted to learn what he knew and how he thought. When you do big things, people want to know how you think. It doesn't just bring success in your realm of influence—it transcends the bounds of what you do. You might be a minister or a baker, but if you're successful, people will want to hear what you have to say about all kinds of realms. Reject failure and embrace the idea of actual biblical success.

 Embrace success.

Before I acquired a plane, I flew on private planes to travel to my meetings. Some people think I shouldn't charter or own a plane. They think I don't belong there. It doesn't bother me. I've embraced it because I know where I belong and I know how I need to operate to get where I'm headed. People's petty thoughts don't matter to me. My mission is what matters to me.

If you don't reject failure and embrace success, you'll subconsciously retreat at the first sign of criticism. I don't care how the religious world thinks I should act, travel, or look. It's not important to me.

I've been given several Rolex watches. I've sown some, I've sold some, and I've worn some. I don't care whether people feel I shouldn't wear them. If the Lord spoke to someone to give me a watch, I'm going to wear it. If my Father gives me a coat of many colors, I'm not hanging it in my closet because my brothers are jealous. People in your family will become upset over your success. Understand that ahead of time and refuse to allow it to affect you.

If Jeffrey Epstein could have a plane to fly friends to his island to molest children, I can use a plane for righteous purposes. You can't make me feel bad about it. In fact, I feel very good about it and I enjoy it. Enjoy your success. Who cares if other people don't like it. God said in Joshua 1, *"I'll give you good success."* Your success is a gift from God. I've struggled before, and I don't ever want to struggle again. Success and prosperity are significant blessings that take the stress out of life.

SECRET 2

UNCOMMON ACHIEVERS ESTABLISH A CLEAR-CUT GOAL

Solomon stated his goal in one sentence—he wanted to build a grand temple for God and a palace for himself, and he did it.

> And Solomon determined to build a house for the name of the Lord, and an house for his kingdom.
>
> — 2 CHRONICLES 2:1 (KJV)

You should be able to express your life's mission in a simple statement. If I asked you what your goal in life is, what would you say? Thousands of businesses and ministries never grow because they don't have a clear-cut goal. Not just a dream—a clear, measurable goal. If I ask a pastor what the goal of their ministry is, I don't want to hear something like, "We want to release the fragrance of worship over our city." That's not a tangible goal. It's language people in prophetic circles like to use, but it's not a goal. If there's no way to determine if you've achieved it, it's not a goal.

Solomon determined to build the Temple to honor the name of the Lord, and a royal palace for himself. Winning one soul at a time is not a goal—it's a course of action. Declaring you want to win one hundred thousand souls is a goal. My father's goal for his ministry is "In dependence upon God, our goal is to lead one million people to a personal relationship with the Lord Jesus Christ." That's a straightforward, clear-cut statement. Billy Graham's mission was "To proclaim the Gospel of Jesus Christ and to equip others to do the same." Another simple, easily understandable statement.

Can you clearly communicate your goal right now? If you can't, no problem. That's why you're reading this book. Take some time and think about it. It's hard to hit a small target, but it's impossible to hit a target you don't have. If you don't have a stated goal for your life, you'll fail to move. When you have a clear-cut goal, you know what you should and shouldn't do. You're aware when an action won't lead toward your end goal. Some things might have value to other people. Some things might need to be done, but they don't need to be done by you. Human trafficking is a terrible thing that needs to be addressed. It's a need, but it's not my calling.

> **Just because there's a need doesn't mean it's your calling.**

Orphans need to be fed and clothed. It's a legitimate ministry. Revival Today sends money to organizations that address this need, but it's not my thing. There are many good causes in the world. There are many things that God told The Church to do, but not everything is my assignment. What is your assignment?

There's a commonly circulated claim that the top three percent of Harvard graduates achieve the most because they wrote their goals down on paper. That study doesn't exist—it's internet fiction. However, a study was conducted that found those who write their goals have a thirty-three percent greater success rate and significantly outproduce those who don't write their goals.[i]

The more tangible and clear-cut you can make your goal, the better your outcome. You should have a goal that could be easily explained to people who aren't Christians. I can explain the value and goal of Revival Today Church and Revival Today's evangelistic ministry to anyone, not just Christians.

SECRET 3

UNCOMMON ACHIEVERS RECEIVE GOD'S STAMP OF APPROVAL

> "I am about to build a Temple to honor the name of the Lord my God. It will be a place set apart to burn fragrant incense before him, to display the special sacrificial bread, and to sacrifice burnt offerings each morning and evening, on the Sabbaths, at new moon celebrations, and at the other appointed festivals of the Lord our God. He has commanded Israel to do these things forever."
>
> — 2 CHRONICLES 2:4

Solomon built the Temple because God instructed him to do so. My dad's mission statement for his ministry begins with "In dependence upon God." Likewise, I'm not doing my own thing. My actions align with what God wants to accomplish on the Earth. I'm not trying to get God to bless something that is of no interest to Him. My mission is linked to

God's mission. Uncommon achievers receive God's stamp of approval on what they pursue. They commit their plans to the Lord.

> Trust in the Lord with all your heart; do not depend on your own understanding. Seek his will in all you do, and he will show you which path to take.
>
> — PROVERBS 3:5-6

SECRET 4

UNCOMMON ACHIEVERS ANNOUNCE THEIR GOAL AND EXPLAIN ITS VALUE AND PURPOSE

Solomon also sent this message to King Hiram at Tyre: "Send me cedar logs as you did for my father, David, when he was building his palace. I am about to build a Temple to honor the name of the Lord my God. It will be a place set apart to burn fragrant incense before him, to display the special sacrificial bread, and to sacrifice burnt offerings each morning and evening, on the Sabbaths, at new moon celebrations, and at the other appointed festivals of the Lord our God. He has commanded Israel to do these things forever."

— 2 CHRONICLES 2:3-4

Suppose you were a pastor attempting to build a church, and some degenerate on the city council decides they don't need another church and opposes your plans. Could you explain why your church is necessary? Can you explain the value and purpose of your goal and dream? I don't mean can you communicate the value it has to you. Can you explain why people should back it and what it will add to the Earth?

Uncommon achievers announce their goals. From its earliest inception, I spoke about the number of people I believed would attend Revival Today Church and the impact it would have on the nation and the world. It would have been simpler to keep my goals to myself. That way, if it didn't happen, nobody would know except me—that's called unbelief. That's not faith, and that's not utilizing the power of life and death that is in my tongue. Leaders announce their goals and get people moving in the same direction.

When we first started the church, two guys in medical scrubs were waiting in line in front of me. One of them turned around, shook my hand, thanked me for taking a stand, and told me he planned bring his extended family to help me get to one thousand people for Resurrection Sunday. I had never met him before. He had never been to the church. So, how did he know? He knew because I announced my goal. When you write the vision and make it plain, other people take it and run with it. That's the importance of communicating your goal and explaining the value and purpose of your life's mission.

SECRET 5

UNCOMMON ACHIEVERS VALUE THE GREATNESS OF THEIR GOALS AND ARE PROUD OF THEM

> "This must be a magnificent Temple because our God is greater than all other gods."
>
> — 2 CHRONICLES 2:5

If you don't see the value in your goal, no one else will see it either. You should have zeal and enthusiasm about your goal. You've already failed if you don't get excited when you talk about it. Some preachers describe their ministries so poorly that no one wants to be a part of it. "We just have a small church. We wanted to build a little place to keep the Gospel light on in our community." That's the opposite of taking pride in your goal—it's belittling it. You don't need to be nauseous in your depiction, but you should value and believe in what you're doing.

You should be able to describe what God put in your heart to accomplish in such a way that people want to help you do it. "Wow, when do you meet? Can I bring my family?" is the type of response you should receive after describing your mission. Our church has an overwhelming number of volunteers. When our church was only three months old, we had more volunteers than members. They're excited about what we're doing, and we make sure to maintain that level of excitement. As a result, the number of volunteers we have continues to grow as our church grows. If I ever hear we're having trouble getting volunteers, I'll know something is wrong. When your goals and ambitions are exciting, people drive long distances, show up early to practice, and prepare for something they want to be part of.

When people come around you, they should develop a desire to be part of what you're doing. After I got married, I didn't want my wife to get a secular job because she wanted to be a part of my mission. My daughter, Camila, wants to be a part of it, too. Not only does my daughter want to help, but she also wants to start right away. She asked me, "Why do I have to go to Bible college? I listen to you all the time. I want to help you. I want to be your Barnabas." She's welcome to change her mind as she gets older, but if she wants to be my Barnabas, that's fine with me.

Stop the self-deprecation. Some people don't have success because they have subconsciously given up on their assignment. You can tell by the way they describe it. Don't be arrogant and leave people wishing you'd shut up about it. But you should have joy, zeal, and infectious enthusiasm when speaking about what God has called you to do, and it should make people want to get involved.

SECRET 6

UNCOMMON ACHIEVERS DEVELOP A DETAILED PLAN

These are the dimensions Solomon used for the foundation of the Temple of God (using the old standard of measurement). It was 90 feet long and 30 feet wide. The entry room at the front of the Temple was 30 feet wide, running across the entire width of the Temple, and 30 feet high. He overlaid the inside with pure gold. He paneled the main room of the Temple with cypress wood, overlaid it with fine gold, and decorated it with carvings of palm trees and chains.

— 2 CHRONICLES 3:3-5

Uncommon achievers develop a detailed plan to accomplish their goal. Solomon didn't just claim he wanted to build a temple and hoped it would appear—he had an extremely detailed plan. Your goal must have a plan, like the directions for arriving at a destination. When you use Google Maps, Waze, or any other navigation system, you must first know your destination. Then, the software devises a plan to get you there. When I travel to preach, I can't just take off and tell the pilot I'll let him know where I want to go once we're in the air. He needs my destination well in advance to develop a flight plan.

Every NFL team starts their training camp by talking about the Super Bowl. No team's goal is to win one more game than last year. It's always to win the Super Bowl, and they prepare for the season by strategizing to accomplish that goal. Once your goal is clear, you can develop a plan to achieve it.

Many people never experience success, and many don't become achievers, let alone uncommon achievers, because they don't have a goal. They have never actually taken the time to decide what they're trying to achieve. Many of those who have a goal lack a detailed plan for achieving that goal. If your goal is to become President of the United States, you must take practical steps toward that destination. You'd need to be affiliated with a political party that can fund your campaign. Just as driving to a particular location requires a plan, becoming the President of the United States (which I do not desire to do) would require me to identify a daily course of action to achieve that goal. If your goal is to have a large business and be one of the end-time millionaires God will raise up, start with incorporating your business and creating a website—otherwise, you're just dreaming.

SECRET 7

UNCOMMON ACHIEVERS ACKNOWLEDGE THEIR LIMITATIONS

"But who can really build him a worthy home? Not even the highest heavens can contain him! So who am I to consider building a Temple for him, except as a place to burn sacrifices to him?"

— 2 CHRONICLES 2:6

I can't do what my media team does. I can't do what Magalis, our executive administrator, does. I can't do the job of Patrick, our financial officer. I could list every person who works for Revival Today, and I can't do what any of them do. If I could, they wouldn't be employed because I would do it.

I can preach. I'm a good preacher. God gave me a gift to preach when I was nineteen. I know how to run a service. I cannot do accounting, graphic design, broadcasting, or set up a microphone. If I needed to hook up a microphone before going on air, I don't know if I could do it by the end of the day, but Nick could do it in under five minutes. Many leaders never make it very far because they want everything to run through them. If you're going to be an uncommon achiever, you can't do everything yourself. Matthew Ashimolowo, the senior pastor of Kingsway International Christian Centre in London, once told a group of pastors that if they handle all the counseling at their churches, it will never grow past two hundred and fifty people. If everyone must come to the senior pastor for counseling, the church will never grow.

When you effectively announce your goal, it should excite people. When it does, let people run with the excitement and be a part of it. Allow them to do their thing unhindered. You will not accomplish much in life if everything must run through you. There are people who God will bring alongside you to help.

I was happy when I learned that one of our church members is an evangelist and planning an outdoor crusade near the church. They never ran it by me, nor did they need to. They plan to get people saved and bring them into the church. Many pastors would insist on being kept in the loop and feel entitled to interrogate someone from their church who was planning to hold a crusade. "Who said you could do that? Are you licensed? I've never ordained you. Are you a part of our ministerial association?" Who cares? Let people run.

SECRET 8

UNCOMMON ACHIEVERS ESTABLISH A REPUTATION OF INTEGRITY

> King Hiram sent this letter of reply to Solomon: "It is because the LORD loves his people that he has made you their king! Praise the Lord, the God of Israel, who made the heavens and the earth! He has given King David a wise son, gifted with skill and understanding, who will build a Temple for the Lord and a royal palace for himself."
>
> — 2 CHRONICLES 2:12

Solomon established a reputation of integrity with all who knew him, including King Hiram. When I announced I was starting a church—I started a church. People moved here before we even had a building because they knew when I said I was starting a church, a church would be started. They know they can trust me. If I say we're doing a crusade, we're doing a crusade. There won't be a story four months later about how things fell through.

Your word should be like God's Word. If you say it, you do it. The Bible says, *"Let your 'yes' be 'yes' and your 'no' be 'no'"* (Matthew 5:37). We live in a culture that no longer values integrity.

 Credibility is currency.

A minister I know announced he was starting a church. The announcement was all over his Instagram. He invested in graphics and rented a building, but after about a year, I noticed he was preaching in other places on Sundays. He never mentioned anything about his church anymore. A friend of mine asked him about it and discovered the minister shut it down, but it was never mentioned—it just faded away. If that minister ever decides to start another church, who in their right mind would be a part of it after he shut down without explanation?

Admit when you're wrong. If I create a battered women's shelter as part of Revival Today and it doesn't work out and the funding falls through, I wouldn't just quietly shut it down. I'd announce that it wasn't something we were called to do, so we're closing it down. Be upfront with people. Don't be shady—tell people the truth. If people can't trust you, they will never support your vision.

I follow a minister on Instagram who's been married three times since I started following him. His other two marriages aren't even mentioned. He had a wife in his Instagram pictures, then she disappeared. There's a gap where no women are in his pictures, and now, there's a new woman with no explanation. Was the other one murdered? Am I going to see her on *Forensic Files*? Where did the other lady go? That's not integrity.

You know who I married; that breeds credibility. I don't appear to be single, but sometimes you see a lady around the studio. That's the opposite of credibility—that's being shady, and it's not a characteristic of uncommon achievers.

Do you pay people on time, or do people have to track you down for money? Uncommon achievers establish a reputation of integrity. If you tell someone you'll send them money, send it. If you owe a bill, pay it on time. If you say you will do something, do it. If you say you're not doing something, don't do it.

SECRET 9

UNCOMMON ACHIEVERS CONSULT OTHER ACHIEVERS

Solomon also sent this message to King Hiram at Tyre: "Send me cedar logs as you did for my father, David, when he was building his palace."

— 2 CHRONICLES 2:3

Solomon consulted other kings about building the Temple. He made an effort to seek out the expertise of other people because uncommon achievers consult other achievers.

If you're a pastor, you should know who the top pastors are. If you're an evangelist, you should know the top evangelists—not who was the best before they died and went to Heaven, but who on Earth has accomplished what you're currently striving to achieve? When we were on a mission to reach one thousand people for Resurrection Sunday, I listened and spoke to pastors with large churches to discover what I didn't know. The first time our church had baby dedications, it brought in eighty extra family members, and many of them were saved that day. I never knew baby dedications drew people to church, so I wanted to discover what else I didn't know about how to attract new people into our church. I also watched Dr. Pastor Paul Enenche's conference on church growth via YouTube, because he pastors the largest church on planet Earth. I am always seeking to learn from the top people in my field.

 Know the top people in your field.

I was told a story about a pastor who had the opportunity to spend time with a very successful minister. He was one of several people in the room listening to the pastor of a very large church. Others in the room asked questions about the ministry, and the small church pastor continued to offer information about his church even though no one asked. At the time, no one knew who he was, so people assumed he also had a large church. Little did they know, his Sunday attendance would have them begging him to shut up.

People love to talk, but you have to discern whether they are worth listening to. Don't listen to just anyone. Listen to high-level achievers in your field of endeavor. If your goal is to have a large YouTube channel, you need to know who has the largest YouTube channel. Research whether they have ever produced anything about how to grow a YouTube channel. Have they ever shared a testimonial of how they started small? Have they provided insight into what caused them to grow?

Most successful people are eager to share their secrets, but they can't find anyone who will listen. Most unsuccessful people happily talk over those more successful than them rather than sit quietly and listen. They seek approval over knowledge and wisdom.

SECRET 10

UNCOMMON ACHIEVERS ESTABLISH A FIRST-CLASS QUALITY STANDARD

> He decorated the walls of the Temple with beautiful jewels and gold from the land of Parvaim. He overlaid the beams, thresholds, walls, and doors throughout the Temple with gold, and he carved figures of cherubim on the walls.
>
> — 2 CHRONICLES 3:6-7

Uncommon achievers set a first-class standard in everything they do. Solomon acquired the best wood on planet Earth just to overlay it with gold. What difference did it make what was under the gold? He could have used plywood, and no one would have seen it. Instead, he used top-of-the-line cedar and covered it with gold. This still fascinates me after all these years. Yet, if Solomon were an American, the basketball court would have been nicer than the Temple built for the Lord. The Temple would have sheetrock walls, and he would have bragged about the good deal he got on the aluminum roof.

I once traveled to preach at a church. I paid my airfare, rented a car, booked a hotel room, and handled all my expenses and accommodations. The pastor of the church needed a six-figure amount of money to move into a new building, and I thought, 'I'm going to give him the money.' I had the money, and I'm always happy to help build churches, so I decided to do it. The pastor knew I preached as soon as the plane landed, so he mentioned he would have food set aside for me when I finished preaching. After the service, I went back to the green room to discover a vegetable tray and a tub of dip. That was it. I decided he could take the money he saved by not buying real food and pay for his own church. That might sound petty, but I hate stinginess with a passion. You will never regret spending money to bless someone. You don't have to think like I do, but my mentality is that if you can't pay thirty dollars to feed me, I'm not dropping $100,000 to help you build your church. It's not about money. I'm not under the impression that I'm some sort of royalty. I'll eat Doritos right out of the bag at my house. I don't care about myself, but show some class.

 Have some class.

Treat people well. What vehicle do you use to pick up guests from the airport? What hotel do you reserve for people when they come to visit? If you entertain them in your home, is it clean?

When I was about twenty-three years old, I was invited to Montreal to preach, and I stayed with an Italian woman named Angie, along with her husband, son, and daughter. Never before or since has anyone treated me as well as she did. She cooked me huge portions of delicious food every day. One morning, I woke up to a plate of eggs with fresh-cut fruit and an Italian flag planted on top. One night, I went out with the church's youth group and came home at 1:30 a.m. She waited for me to return and cooked me a steak and vegetables. Back then, I wore baggy suits like most Americans, but Angie brought me to Signor Terry, a suit shop in Montreal, and bought me a suit, ties, and dress socks. She was not a wealthy woman, but she made sure I looked my best when I was preaching. I told her I had never been treated this well in my life. She said in her Italian accent, "The Bible says to treat people as you would treat Jesus. I've tried to treat you as I would treat Jesus if He were staying in my home." This happened over two decades ago, and I still think about it. That's how much of an impression it left on me.

At Revival Today, I ensure every guest speaker we host is treated extremely well. We give them a large sum of money in addition to the offering, and they receive high-quality accommodations from the moment their flight lands. I want to set a new standard. I'm going to be the first church—assuming there's not one already—that sends a plane to pick up guest speakers and return them home, and I will put them in the nicest hotel in the city. I will treat people the way I wish people would have treated me when I started in evangelism. If you come to eat at my church, you'll receive a first-class meal. Everything is top-notch.

Try wearing a disguise and walk into your church to see how you're greeted. Some churches have ushers waiting to tell you where to park as soon as you pull in. They have an umbrella for you and escort you inside. In other churches, no one is in the parking lot. When you walk into the church, no one greets you. It's as if no one even cares you're there. You have to figure out who the pastor is and where to find him. There's no class. Most people were raised with no class. You must begin to break away from your upbringing and live differently. Follow the Angie Principle: treat people like you would treat Jesus. *"Whatever you do to the least of these, my brethren, you've done it to me"* (Matthew 25:40).

Most Americans need to step up their class because overall, Americans tend to have low class. They treat people poorly. I've never been treated better than I have by churches in third-world nations. They've gone out of their way to treat me like gold. You would never go to India and be served on paper plates. I've eaten in people's homes in the slums of India. One family had only peanuts to eat. They roasted them and put them on nice, handmade plates with cloth napkins. They were classy peanuts. Meanwhile, Americans with plenty of money serve guests on Dixie paper plates—it's abysmal. How can anyone justify serving a church guest with paper plates and plastic forks? What are you saving the nice utensils for?

Pastors, what does your children's room smell like? What does your church smell like? What does it look like when people walk in? Take a walk through your sanctuary and see how many stains are on the pews. How long will you keep that orange carpet from 1979 with grape juice stains? It doesn't cost money to vacuum your church. Run an air purifier so it doesn't smell like mold. Install automatic air fresheners to spray a pleasant scent.

If you're in ministry, it wouldn't be the worst idea to stay at a Four Seasons hotel as a reconnaissance trip to see how they operate and treat guests. It's the little details that set them apart. When you stay at a five-star hotel, you're treated extremely well from the moment you arrive. No one is allowed to respond with, "We don't have that," or "I can't do that." However, if you stay at a two-star hotel and ask for a latte, they'd have no problem telling you there's a diner three blocks away—not at a five-star hotel. You could ask the maid for a latte, and she'd quickly find someone to bring you one. Nothing is ever a no. Everyone treats you well. Why should there be high-class hospitality at secular hotels and casinos but not at churches?

One advantage I had before starting Revival Today Church was that I had traveled to churches for twenty-one years. I've seen the bad, the mediocre, the good, and I've seen the amazing. It has allowed me to adopt the best practices from other churches into our ministry at Revival Today.

When our church first began growing, people had to park pretty far and walk in the cold. I was looking out my window on the third floor before church started, and I saw older people with canes walking two hundred yards to church. That didn't sit well with me because that's not class. So, we bought two eight-seater golf carts to shuttle people. I can't change the weather, but I can get a golf cart with a roof and turn an eight-minute walk into a forty-second fun ride.

My grandfather used to say this about class: "Some people have it. Some people can't spell it." Some people have money without class, and others have little money but have a great deal of class. Class isn't about money—it's a mentality. Being a bum is a mentality, and having class is a mentality. Bus ministries that pick up kids from trailer parks or ghettos to take them to church often stink, but they shouldn't because it doesn't cost a lot of money to buy soap and wash your children.

It's people's lack of care for clothes that makes them look poor. Sometimes, I see people and wonder, 'What are you saving your good clothes for?' People meet the President at the White House wearing cargo pants. What are you saving your suits for? To meet leaders from other galaxies? Your attention to detail, not the worth of your clothes, determines your level of class.

Back when the magazine wasn't just for homosexuals, *Gentlemen's Quarterly* featured a man wearing a five-thousand-dollar untailored suit and a guy wearing a three-hundred-dollar tailored suit. The guy with a $300 suit looked far superior to the guy in the $5,000 suit. It doesn't cost money to iron your clothes, so they don't look like you keep them in the glove compartment of your car. Have class like Solomon. Small things make the difference between mediocre and excellent.

SECRET 11

UNCOMMON ACHIEVERS ACKNOWLEDGE THOSE WHO HELP THEM

Uncommon achievers employ the principles of thanksgiving and gratitude. Solomon wrote letters acknowledging those who helped him and his father by name. Do you have a thank-you system? I once sent an offering to a very famous preacher, and he called and left a voicemail requesting that I call him back so he could thank me personally. The offering I sent was a decent sum, but I'm sure he receives way more money than that. He didn't send a letter or a book—he called me personally and left his home number so he could thank me. Uncommon achievers are uncommon thanksgivers.

I'm sure there are hundreds of unknown ministers with small to mid-sized ministries who would receive a ten-thousand-dollar seed and never think of contacting anyone in return to thank them. No letter, phone call, or acknowledgment whatsoever, but somehow, when one of the top ministries on the planet—busier than all others put together—receives a ten-thousand-dollar seed, the minister calls and leaves his home phone number requesting a call back to express thanks.

If someone were to give you a hundred dollars, would you just say thank you, and they'd never hear from you again? Would you send them a card? Would you call? Do you thank people who have helped you in life?

Maintaining a mentality of thanksgiving will keep you from becoming discouraged. If you're always focused on who has been a help, you won't have time to think about who has hurt you. If you don't give thanks, your thoughts will revolve around who you thought should have helped you. You'll become preoccupied with wealthy people who haven't helped you as you see fit. If you don't thank people who have helped you, you'll become a complainer. You'll find yourself upset with the people who have helped you for not helping you more.

No one owes you anything, and no one owes me anything. If somebody attending my church makes eleven million dollars a year, they don't owe me a dollar. They don't have to give anything in the offering. That's between them and God.

Make a list of ten people who have helped you in life and do it today. Maybe your mom is on that list, or an elementary school teacher, or a youth pastor. If you're in the ministry, it might be a preacher or ministry God used to help or leave an impression on you. Have you ever thanked them? Have you ever thanked your youth pastor or your children's pastor? How about your Sunday school teacher? The one who taught you the Word of God, who's now in their eighties, sitting somewhere thinking no one cares they taught Sunday school for thirty-five years. After you make that list, write them a thank-you letter or a card. Don't allow the people who have helped you spend their days in tears, discouraged by the Devil, thinking no one knows or cares who they are. When you sow encouragement, you will reap encouragement—what you sow, you reap.

I'm not very good at remembering to thank people, but thankfully, I have my wife, Adalis. She does a great job. When someone gives to our ministry, I always announce what I will send as a thank you. It's not that anyone gives strictly for that reason, although at times, I have. I know what it's like to send one thousand dollars to a ministry with just eleven hundred dollars to your name and not even know if anyone got it or cared. It's nice to know your gift is appreciated. Part of the fun of giving is seeing the person's face when you give to them. When I took my daughter to a hockey game, I got her an ice cream popsicle from a Dairy Queen stand without her asking. When I handed it to her, she lit up. That's the fun of giving.

SECRET 12

UNCOMMON ACHIEVERS INVOLVE AS MANY PEOPLE AS POSSIBLE IN THEIR ENDEAVORS

Solomon took a census of all foreigners in the land of Israel, like the census his father had taken, and he counted 153,600. He assigned 70,000 of them as common laborers, 80,000 as quarry workers in the hill country, and 3,600 as foremen.

— 2 CHRONICLES 2:17-18

Uncommon achievers involve as many people in their endeavors as possible, and they spare no expense to realize their vision. Yet, insecurity and frugality are two of the most common things that prevent people from allowing others to be involved in their endeavors. I don't want to know where Revival Today Church would be right now if I had decided to be the general contractor on the build-out of the church's property to save money. It might have opened in 2026. What if I decided to design my own graphics to save money instead of hiring a team? What if I set up my camera and turned it on myself to broadcast just to save money? When your central focus is saving money, you don't involve others. Trying to do everything yourself keeps you small, but if you hire the right people, their work will more than pay for itself. Don't hold yourself back by being cheap.

Insecure people are threatened by other people who want to help, but if you're intimidated by other people, you'll never be an uncommon achiever. Unfortunately, most people are extremely insecure. If they don't get the credit, they'd rather something not get done than allow someone else to receive recognition.

I've preached for pastors who were upset when their members attended my revival meeting but didn't often show up to midweek services. Why do they care? Your people are in church. I'm leaving and they're going to stay. They gave in *your* offering. Not everything has to revolve around you. I rarely talk to a pastor about what I've learned from Bishop David Oyedepo without hearing, "Well, we do that here too." They can't celebrate anyone else. Everything has to pertain to them and their idea.

When people complain they don't have enough volunteers for something, I question whether it's a volunteer problem. Often, what they've been asked to do feels unimportant, so it doesn't attract anyone because of how it's presented. It's possible to make something important seem trivial. For instance, if you needed people to help with your children's ministry, you could announce on Sunday, "We need people to watch the children during the revival meeting." Would you want to help watch the children if you heard that? Instead, what if you said, "I believe the children in this church will be world-changers. If you were impacted by a Sunday school teacher, you can attest to the significance of Sunday school in the lives of our youth. Now it's your turn to impact our children the way you were impacted." When you put it that way, you might end up with too many volunteers.

When God sends you people, turn them loose to excel at what they do. Let them run with your vision. Give as many people the opportunity to be involved in the vision as possible. If you have something worth being involved in, there will be people who want to be involved in it. So, give them direction and let them run.

SECRET 13

UNCOMMON ACHIEVERS ORGANIZE AND DELEGATE RESPONSIBILITIES

Uncommon achievers organize and delegate responsibilities. They don't try to do everything. Solomon didn't just delegate responsibilities—he was also well-organized.

Our first church building was constructed in under two months, but I never once showed up with a hard hat, directing people on how to work with drywall. When visitors ask where we ordered our chairs or sound system from, I can't answer them. I have no idea because I wasn't involved in any of that. Those tasks were delegated because uncommon achievers organize and delegate responsibility. If you know how much you've paid for every single item in your business or ministry, that might be a problem, and if you continue that way, you won't grow. A time will come when you'll need to take your hands off and let people run. Do you think Joel Osteen knows what Lakewood Church's electric bill was this month? Small-minded people have their hands in everything.

There was a brief point in our ministry when people looked stressed. Our office had always been a very joyous place, but suddenly, there wasn't much joy around the office. When we started the church and moved to a new building, I thought people were trying to adjust to the new surroundings, but that wasn't it. It turns out that when we added new church responsibilities, it caused a workflow problem. Magalis, our head administrator, would send out a text to the staff about tasks that needed to be completed, and four people would end up doing the same task. People weren't clear about their assignments. The team met and reorganized the workflow, and now everyone knows their assignment and who they report to. Delegating tasks and providing clarity on who does what ensures that our work environment is organized and full of joy.

SECRET 14

UNCOMMON ACHIEVERS USE THE EXPERTISE OF SPECIALISTS

"I am sending you a master craftsman named Huram-abi, who is extremely talented. His mother is from the tribe of Dan in Israel, and his father is from Tyre. He is skillful at making things from gold, silver, bronze, and iron, and he also works with stone and wood. He can work with purple, blue, and scarlet cloth and fine linen. He is also an engraver and can follow any design given to him. He will work with your craftsmen and those appointed by my lord David, your father."

— 2 CHRONICLES 2:13-14

Solomon used the expertise of specialists to build the Temple. He didn't watch YouTube tutorials on how to engrave gold to save money. We enlisted the top sound engineer in the world to lay out the sound for our church and studio. Top churches bring in top sound engineers and production teams to work with their worship team and ministry staff for Christmas productions. Use specialists, and you won't regret it.

In this day and age, no one should be confined by their geographic location. You could live in rural Arkansas and fly someone in from New York to train your staff. You're not limited by what and who is around you. You can network across the globe. Call trade schools and request their best students. Invest in excellence. Don't feel threatened by specialists. Seek them out and use their expertise.

SECRET 15

UNCOMMON ACHIEVERS MAKE CONTRACT DETAILS AND EXPECTATIONS VERY CLEAR

Uncommon achievers make the details, expectations, and descriptions of all contracts very clear. In chapters two and three of 2 Chronicles, Solomon clearly outlined the details and descriptions of all contracts and expectations for those he employed to build the Temple. Business is not a friendship. Don't trust anyone, not even yourself. Protect yourself from other people; you don't know them. I've lost count of how many Christians have suffered embezzlement or other problems because of excessive trust and a lack of clear contractual expectations. Don't be slothful in business. It's not a game. Don't take your life, ministry, or business lightly. We require our staff to sign a non-disclosure agreement. If anyone left our ministry and wrote a tell-all book, they would be sued for a great deal of money because they signed the agreement. They cannot talk about anything that goes on here.

All communication must be in writing. There was a time when if someone asked you for something, you could get away with saying they never asked you for anything. Written expectations remove all the guesswork. Every staff member at Revival Today knows the time they're supposed to be at work, what's expected of them, and what they need to accomplish in the day. They understand their specific tasks because we have written all this so there is clarity on what they are supposed to do.

Communication solves ninety percent of disagreements and anger. One conversation can solve most disagreements and problems. Yet people will read this while simultaneously stewing over something an employee didn't know they were supposed to do because it wasn't clearly communicated.

SECRET 16

UNCOMMON ACHIEVERS COMPENSATE AND REWARD THOSE WHO ASSIST THEM IN ACHIEVING THEIR GOALS

> So Hiram supplied as much cedar and cypress timber as Solomon desired. **In return**, Solomon sent him an annual payment of 100,000 bushels of wheat for his household and 110,000 gallons of pure olive oil.
>
> — 1 KINGS 5:10-11

Uncommon achievers reward those who assist them in achieving their goals. There's a cliché in business that "leaders eat last." You can see this principle with Abraham when he led men to battle. He paid a tithe to Melchizedek, and then he paid all his men. He didn't take all the money for himself. I can't speak for business because I'm not in that world, but ignorance of this secret causes many ministries to flatline—everything goes to the guy at the top, and the helpers get nothing.

In Pentecostal circles, it was common to be asked to "live by faith." In reality, being asked to live by faith meant they weren't going to pay you. That has nothing to do with faith. It's anti-faith because Abraham is the father of our faith, and he paid his men.

Uncommon achievers reward those who assist them in achieving their goals, but common losers keep everything for themselves and don't pay a fair wage. There are people at churches working twenty-plus hours per week who were roped in as volunteers. Their help is expected, and in return, they receive a fifty-dollar gift card to Starbucks at Christmas for their trouble. That's wrong. As a leader, you're hurting yourself along with your business or ministry if you treat people this way.

I hope I can get you to cross a bridge in your mind that trying to get someone to help you for free hurts you. You're hurting your mind, your mentality, your reputation, and people's desire to help you in the future.

In an attempt to follow the golden rule of the Bible, I probably overpay people, but the Bible is clear: *"Do unto others as you would have others do unto you"* (Luke 6:31).

My wife went on a trip and left me with sole custody of my daughter for forty-eight hours. I brought her with me to broadcast *Check the News*, and when we finished, I asked her if she had eaten, as if she could have run out to fix a meal for herself—she was nine. Obviously, she hadn't had dinner. I was with her the whole time, and she hadn't eaten since lunch at school. I took her to Primanti Brothers for dinner. They had just raised their prices, but it was still insanely cheap—our bill was twelve dollars. I ordered five boneless wings, and she ordered a kid's pizza. She drank a Sprite, and I had water. A twenty percent tip on a twelve-dollar bill is two dollars and forty cents, but our waiter was extremely nice—probably in his early twenties. He told me a story about the time he took his nephew out for a late dinner because he was caught up doing something. I arrived after 11:30 p.m., and he could have told me, "We close at midnight, bro. The kitchen is closed." He didn't even rush me to order. He was completely unbothered by the timing of my arrival, so there was no way I could leave him two dollars.

I'm telling you this to illustrate the golden rule. I thought to myself, 'What would I hope someone might do for me in this situation?' Not two dollars and forty cents, that's for sure. Then I thought about how many people probably stiffed him that day, so I left him a fifty-dollar tip. As I walked Camila to our vehicle, he busted out the door and said, "Thank you so much. You made my night. I really appreciate that." I never told him I was the pastor of the church next door, but someone will. Someday, when someone makes false claims about me, he'll remember me and respond, "Oh, him? No, no, no, he's a good guy."

My first job while in Bible school was an internship as the youth pastor of a Spirit-filled Presbyterian church—whatever that is—and they paid me fifty dollars a week. Even back in the 90s, that wasn't much. I often took very low-paying jobs after graduating from Bible college, so I know what it's like to struggle. I know what it's like to have a wife in pain from a toothache and have to settle for two Advil because we couldn't afford to go to the dentist. Today, she just says, "Hey, I'm going to the dentist," and I don't even ask how much it costs because it doesn't matter. When people claim they're not interested in success, I understand how their brains work because I've had success, and I've had the opposite of success, but I'm telling you, success is much better. Here's a novel revelation for Christians: success is better than failure. It's one or the other; pick which you want. God said He'd give you good success if He had His way.

Pastor Rodney Howard-Browne says that sometimes God puts you around someone to take that person out of you. I think I've been around so many people who shortchanged their ministerial staff that it took that tendency out of me. I decided when I was twenty-three that when I was in charge, the people who worked for me would be blessed. That guy at Primanti Brothers doesn't work for me, but he helped me accomplish my goal of feeding my daughter, so I blessed him too.

How would you want to be treated if you were your youth pastor? In some ministries, the only way to receive a raise is if you get married or have a child. Everything is need-based. That's socialism. Christians say they don't like communism, but they run their ministries like communists. All salaries are need-based. That's welfare. Compensation should be performance-based. If someone's married with six kids and they suck, they shouldn't be paid as well as a single person who does a great job.

During COVID, everyone in our ministry received raises and bonuses. When COVID hit, it looked as if we were going to be arrested. When I say "we," I mean me. It looked like a page out of Canada and Australia's playbook. I'm sure it was their goal. We were able to play a small hand in keeping that from happening. I decided if we were going to get arrested anyway, I would run my mouth and speak out against government overreach until they took me in. I decided to curse it and expose it, and I felt the Lord say, "Deal with people's spirits in the day and deal with their minds at night."

We hosted *Check the News* at night. When he was behind the green desk, Pastor Rodney Howard-Browne asked me to come broadcast with him for three or four hours a night. My staff was broadcasting with me from 11:00 a.m. to 12:30 p.m. Then, working as I preached from 2:00 p.m. to 3:30 p.m., then continued to work while I went live with Pastor Rodney from 7:00 p.m. to 11:00 p.m. Then they closed out the night with *Check the News* from 11:30 p.m. to 1:00 a.m., and returned to do Pastor Kofi's morning prayer broadcast at 6:00 a.m.

They were happy to do it, but just because someone is happy to do something doesn't mean they should be punished for it. Do you only pay people if they look miserable? A pleasant disposition should make you want to pay people more. They were working a lot. We were all living at the studio and eating meals together. Because we were on the air so often and almost everyone else's ministries were shut down, giving to our ministry skyrocketed. I started passing out bonuses left and right. I gave everyone an extra five thousand dollars for their hard work.

That's how to keep morale high. It keeps people excited about the vision. If you put people in poverty, they won't stay excited about your actions. You're only hurting yourself by trying to get a good deal on paying the people who help you.

I ordered a pricey custom item from a friend in Pittsburgh. He made it and did a great job. When he told me the price, I added an extra thousand dollars. He didn't understand why I wasn't negotiating lower. I refused to leave the store until he rang it up for the higher price. When he asked me why, I told him, "You're my friend. Should I use the fact that we're friends to pay you less, or because you're my friend, should I look to bless you?" He said, "I wish more people thought like you."

Abel, my brother-in-law, did all the construction on our office building. Should I have asked him to do it for free? Should I have asked him to give me a discount? Why not pay him more? Why not pay him the standard? Why are people in the Body of Christ always looking to take advantage of people? Stop trying to get people to do stuff for free.

Doing your best doesn't feel good when people don't care. That's why it's important to combine compensation and reward with the golden rule. Put yourself in someone else's position. In the ministry, doubly so. I will never allow an unsaved person to work for free. Many people offer to do things like landscaping for free. Even my barber, whom I led to the Lord, cuts priests' hair for free. He thought I was a priest, so my haircut was free, but I gave him one hundred dollars every time. The Catholic priest took the free haircut, but I'll give you one guess who he goes to church with.

Unsaved people agree to do things for free for churches to appease their conscience. I won't let them do anything for free because I don't want their conscience eased. I don't want them to feel like they've bought their salvation when what they need is to start going to church. I'd rather pay and tip until the person feels moved to come and get saved. I don't want a deal. I want people to go to Heaven. I don't want people to feel like Al Capone. He thought because he had built a few churches in Chicago, he was entitled to break the law. You hurt your endeavor by not compensating people who help you. Compensate people well. When you're cheap and stingy, you'll have a high staff turnover and eventually lose every person God sends to help you.

Magalis, my wife's twin sister, manages our entire administrative operation. She receives an executive salary. People will rise and sink to the level you pay them. If someone paid me volunteer wages and threw in a gift card once a year, I wouldn't even shower before I came to work. I'd arrive when I felt like it and work until I felt like stopping. People rise to the level you treat them, but in the same respect, if you notice someone sleeping on the job or not performing, fire them.

Another principle from the Bible illustrates this point: *"The laborer is worthy of his hire"* (Luke 10:7). It's unscriptural not to pay someone for their work. The Bible also states: *"Do not muzzle an ox while it's treading out the grain"* (1 Timothy 5:18). Hire quality people and pay them what they deserve.

Things should be better in God's Kingdom than in the world. If you hire someone away from an executive position to come work for your ministry, it should be a step up financially, not a step down. Stop trying to get deals at the expense of other people. Don't force people to use their faith because you won't use yours.

SECRET 17

UNCOMMON ACHIEVERS KEEP THE ENTHUSIASM AND GREATNESS OF THEIR PROJECT ALIVE

Then Solomon said, "My father, David, wanted to build this Temple to honor the name of the Lord, the God of Israel. But the Lord told him, 'You wanted to build the Temple to honor my name. Your intention is good, but you are not the one to do it. One of your own sons will build the Temple to honor me.' "And now the Lord has fulfilled the promise he made, for I have become king in my father's place, and now I sit on the throne of Israel, just as the Lord promised. I have built this Temple to honor the name of the Lord, the God of Israel. And I have prepared a place there for the Ark, which contains the covenant that the Lord made with our ancestors when he brought them out of Egypt."

— 1 KINGS 8:17-21

Uncommon achievers keep the enthusiasm and greatness of their project alive. Solomon kept the enthusiasm and greatness of his project alive by telling the people working for him why they were building a Temple. He explained it was an assignment from God. His father started it, and he was going to finish it. In the verses above, Solomon was speaking to the people he enlisted to help him. In the previous chapter, Solomon valued the greatness of his goal and was proud of it. There's a difference between valuing your goal and maintaining enthusiasm for your goal because things will get stale if you let them. People forget the purpose behind the task at hand. As the leader, it's your job to keep genuine enthusiasm alive for your mission. Remind people of the vision that excited them in the beginning. Remind people why they're here.

Some churches feel stale—no one's excited. The church reception office feels like a funeral home.

> The vine is dried up, and the fig tree languisheth; the pomegranate tree, the palm tree also, and the apple tree, even all the trees of the field, are withered: because joy is withered away from the sons of men.
>
> — JOEL 1:12 (KJV)

The harvests failed to produce *because joy withered from the hearts of men*. Part of producing is maintaining the joy and enthusiasm of your task. Nehemiah 8:10 says, "*The joy of the Lord is your strength.*" Joy brings strength. That's why joy and productivity go hand in hand. The day I dread teaching and writing books is the day my ministry is over. Some ministers dread preaching at their own church. If the leader dreads going to church, you can be sure the people dread going too. People enjoy being around happy people, and they want to give in a joyful atmosphere.

Jesse Duplantis has one of the richest ministries on the planet. Offering times in his meetings are always happy times. He doesn't berate people into giving. People laugh as they give.

We don't go through the motions at Revival Today Church. We're reaching and climbing with enthusiasm. Keep the enthusiasm and greatness of your project alive. Make sure your staff and those who help you achieve your mission know and understand your vision.

SECRET 18

UNCOMMON ACHIEVERS ONLY HIRE HAPPY PEOPLE

And she said to the king, It was a true report that I heard in mine own land of thy acts and of thy wisdom. Howbeit I believed not the words, until I came, and mine eyes had seen it: and, behold, the half was not told me: thy wisdom and prosperity exceedeth the fame which I heard. Happy are thy men, happy are these thy servants, which stand continually before thee, and that hear thy wisdom.

— 1 KINGS 10:6-8 (KJV)

Solomon only hired happy people because uncommon achievers only hire happy people. If you're sad in my ministry, you're fired. Something is wrong. When the Queen of Sheba met Solomon's staff, she marveled at how happy his servants were. Maybe in her palace, everyone was very serious because they didn't know if they were going to get beheaded, but it wasn't like that in Solomon's palace. People were laughing it up.

It's incredible how many great ministers of powerful ministries—with miracles—were later discovered to be living in sin. After finding out, Adalis and I always say to each other, "You know what, though? They were never happy." The Bible says, *"Happy are the people whose God is the Lord"* (Psalm 144:15). When someone is sad, their salvation is questionable. If the Bible says those whose God is the Lord are happy and that in His presence there's fullness of joy, then someone walking around sad needs help. Get them help and get them delivered so they can be happy again. I don't mean members of the congregation. I'm referring to the people who work with you.

People who don't even attend our church come to our office. People like being here. Our staff is happy. I've heard many people remark about it. No one is tense. You can tell right away if staff is underpaid because they seem to have the weight of the world on them—they're not happy.

Uncommon achievers only hire happy people. I would rather have a happy, unsaved person working for our ministry than an unhappy Christian because I wouldn't believe they were Christians. If you're continually sad, I don't believe you're a Christian.

When David's wives and family were kidnapped, he encouraged himself in the Lord the same day. He put on the garment of praise for the spirit of heaviness. If you want to be miserable, hire unhappy people; it's true in ministry and business.

How can you get more joy? Hang around joyful people. It's the same way you receive anything—through impartation, so guard your company.

I minister to depressed people, but I don't hang around them. Those you minister to and those around you continually are two different groups. If I see someone continually sad, I assume they're in sin. *"The blessing of the Lord, it maketh rich, and he addeth no sorrow with it"* (Proverbs 10:22 KJV).

HOW TO STAY JOYFUL

1. Control your atmosphere. You never feel good while talking about bad things.

Don't listen to music written by suicidal people. Keep things around you that bring you joy. Keep a photo album on your phone just to remind you of great memories. Take pictures of the great times you've had. There are things you can look at that immediately snap you from a good mood to a sad, bad, or angry mood. Talk about a good memory or about your dreams. Get a picture of where you want to go in life and hang it up. What you put before your eyes matters. The eyes are the window to the soul. Put pictures up that make you smile and laugh.

2. Say the right words, and the right feelings will follow. Don't wait until you feel good to say good things. Say good things, and good feelings will follow. Let your words, not your feelings, be the engine that runs the locomotive. What you think about influences your mood.

When Adalis is away and Camilla feels sad because she misses her mother, I don't say, "Mommy will be home tomorrow." I ask her to tell me the five best memories we have together. Her eyes always light up as she begins to tell me about the time I surprised her with a trip to Disney. The rehearsal of your fond memories contains all the good emotions you felt when you experienced them for the first time. Sometimes, thinking about and planning a vacation is as much fun as the vacation itself. It's enjoyable to research activities and restaurants on Yelp. What you meditate on will control your mood. What are your five best memories? Don't hang a photo in your living room of your brother who passed away. Put it somewhere you can look at it when you feel like it, not in a place that snaps you out of a good mood every time you pass by.

Either you will control your mood or outside factors will influence your mood—you choose. I've learned how to control my mood. It took me a long time, but I'm pretty good at it now. I'm amazed by how many people in the ministry allow one negative comment on their Facebook page to dominate their actions and thoughts for the next five days. Most people are slaves to the opinions of others. That's no way to maintain joy.

Assess your staff. Are they happy? If they're not, give them twenty-four hours to get happy; if they don't, give them twenty-four hours to get out. Replace them with somebody happy. It will immediately enhance your ministry or business. There could be someone on your staff holding up your harvest, and you wouldn't even know it. Walk through the front door of your church on Sunday or your business on Monday in disguise, and see how you're treated when you walk in. Remember, uncommon achievers hire happy people and reproduce themselves in others. So, an uncommon achiever needs to be happy and surrounded by happy people.

SECRET 19

UNCOMMON ACHIEVERS ESTABLISH A SCHEDULE FOR THEIR GOALS AND BEGIN WORKING

If you wait for perfect conditions, you will never get anything done.

— ECCLESIASTES 11:4 (TLB)

He that observeth the wind shall not sow; and he that regardeth the clouds shall not reap.

— ECCLESIASTES 11:4 (KJV)

Uncommon achievers establish a project schedule and begin working. Solomon established a project schedule and got to work.

> **At some point, you must stop preparing and start doing.**

Some people are always getting ready—always planning. At some point, you must stop planning and start doing. Uncommon achievers get moving.

A dream turns into a vision when you put a date on it. Our church building on Patton Drive was given to us. As I was leaving *Check the News* one night, the previous owner of the building was in the parking lot. He said, "I want to tell you something. If you guys hadn't moved on the building the way you did, I never would've given it to you. I would've had you pay for it. When I mentioned you could start working on it, you had people in there the next day. I saw how serious you were, that's when I decided to give it to you." I'm not trying to pat myself on the back, but if most people were given a building, it would sit empty for months. We've put over a million dollars into it, even though it was free. Chairs aren't free, carpeting isn't free, lighting isn't free, and electricity and wiring aren't free—nothing is free. Most people wait to work on a property that has been given to them while they try to raise money. Get moving. At some point, you must stop preparing and start doing. There will always be things you require to realize your vision, but the old saying is: "The provision is on the battlefield." That does not mean you stop learning—it means you don't stop once you feel you've surpassed your abilities. Uncommon achievers establish a project schedule and begin working.

SECRET 20

UNCOMMON ACHIEVERS ESTABLISH ORDER AND FLOW IN EVERYTHING THEY DO

When the queen of Sheba realized how wise Solomon was, and when she saw the palace he had built, she was overwhelmed. She was also amazed at the food on his tables, the organization of his officials and their splendid clothing, the cup-bearers and their robes, and the burnt offerings Solomon made at the Temple of the Lord. She exclaimed to the king, "Everything I heard in my country about your achievements and wisdom is true! I didn't believe what was said until I arrived here and saw it with my own eyes.

— 2 CHRONICLES 9:3-6

Solomon established order and flow in everything he did.

Proper order and flow are byproducts of implementing effective systems. Your business or ministry needs systems. Who fields your phone calls? What's the workflow when someone calls your office? What's the workflow for mail that comes to your office? How do you accommodate visitors? Who greets them? What is your daily workflow?

Systems are better than goals. I take one day off each week because the Bible says to chill. God has a Sabbath system. If you work every day, you'll burn out. When you take one day to replenish, you're honoring God's system, but outside of your one day of rest, you should have systems that lead to a productive workflow.

 Systems are better than goals.

If I decided to broadcast on YouTube only when I felt like it, I would probably end up doing it four times a month. Instead, I have a system in place. I broadcast Tuesday through Friday mornings at 11:00 a.m. on weeks when I'm not traveling to preach. We host noon prayer—whether or not I feel like praying—from noon to 1:00 p.m.

Before you know it, this year will be over. If you don't put a system in place, the years will slip through your fingers, and you'll be in the exact place three years from now as you are today, with a bunch of unrealized dreams. Create a daily flow for yourself to prevent that from becoming your reality.

I put my phone on Do Not Disturb when I go to sleep at night, and I take it off when I wake up in the morning. I refuse to allow my day to be dictated by a panicked phone call. Have systems and respect other people's systems. I have someone who schedules visitors and engagements. That's not my strength. If I were responsible for scheduling appointments, I'd be consistently triple-booked. That's not my gift. I recognize I'm awful at that, so I've implemented a system to ensure it's done competently.

Solomon had great people working with him, and he made sure they were well organized. I've modeled our ministry operations after Solomon. Everyone knows their job. We just hired our seventy-first full-time staff. We have a staff member who runs the floor. It's not his job to do anything else but media, design, and other technical things. I hired Rom to run our broadcasts. Nick produces excellent media. That's his job. We hired a receptionist because every time the phone rang, someone was pulled away from their tasks to answer it. Now, we pay someone a full-time salary to answer the phone and direct the calls to the correct department, so phone calls don't reduce productivity. That's a lot of money to pay someone just to answer phones, but the money we pay a receptionist allows others to be more productive. It will enable the ministry to produce things that generate more than a receptionist's salary.

If I decide to hire a chauffeur to drive me where I need to go, it's an added $50,000 expense, considering I can drive myself. But if I hired someone to drive me to and from my house while I used the hour and fifteen minutes to study, write letters, and do other mission-critical tasks, I could outproduce that chauffeur's salary.

Uncommon achievers establish an orderly workflow for everything they do; common underachievers don't have an orderly workflow. They're available to hang out at a moment's notice. I used to be the person who could hang out on a whim. Now, if someone were to call me up to tell me they were visiting Pittsburgh, chances are I wouldn't even be in the state of Pennsylvania, and if I was home, I'd probably be preaching. I'm sure some people who knew me twenty years ago would be surprised to hear me say I'm unavailable, but I now have systems in place. Establishing good systems keeps leaders from burning out. Focus on your gifting and spend as much time as possible doing only that—have others do the rest.

A wealthy businessman pulled me aside and told me he was concerned about how hard I was working. I told him I don't work hard. Speaking is not working; it's what God called me to do. Speaking, praying, and preaching are all easy—these things are covered by the anointing. But if I had to do the prep work for guests, run errands, and perform other tasks outside my gifting, I would burn out.

The old saying goes, "Hard work never killed anybody; wrong work kills people." Understand and stick with your assignment, and utilize the people God brings into your life. Don't feel bad about it.

SECRET 21

UNCOMMON ACHIEVERS ARE LIFETIME STUDENTS

S olomon was a lifelong student. Uncommon achievers are lifetime students. They're always collecting wisdom that pertains to the assignment God called them to fulfill.

> God gave Solomon very great wisdom and understanding, and knowledge as vast as the sands of the seashore. In fact, his wisdom exceeded that of all the wise men of the East and the wise men of Egypt. He was wiser than anyone else, including Ethan the Ezrahite and the sons of Mahol— Heman, Calcol, and Darda. His fame spread throughout all the surrounding nations. He composed some 3,000 proverbs and wrote 1,005 songs. He could speak with authority about all kinds of plants, from the great cedar of Lebanon to the tiny hyssop that grows from cracks in a wall. He

could also speak about animals, birds, small creatures, and fish. And kings from every nation sent their ambassadors to listen to the wisdom of Solomon.

— 1 KINGS 4:29-34

> **Very few things pertain to your assignment.**

A businesswoman once commented, "My husband is impressed by how you speak without notes and quote the Bible all the time without having to look at anything." Well, that's my job. The Bible is alive, but it's static in the sense that the book of 1 Peter will always have five chapters, and the verses contained in each chapter will never change. When I wake up in the morning, there won't be a sixth chapter in 1 Peter; it's the same as the day before.

If stock traders can memorize every Dow ticker symbol and can name the CEOs of every Fortune 500 company, a minister should know the Bible forward and backward. Bishop David Oyedepo is an excellent example of someone who knows the Bible. When Kenneth Hagin was still on the Earth, he quoted one scripture after another from memory. Truthfully, I should know the Scriptures better than I do.

Uncommon achievers consider themselves lifetime students. They understand they'll never learn everything, but they strive to do so. Have you ever been around someone who seems to know about any subject you bring up? College football, art galleries, you name it—they know about *too many* things. Become a specialist in your field of knowledge. There should be a subject you're very knowledgeable about, and your knowledge should always be fresh and up-to-date.

Pilots must undergo retraining. You don't want to just be knowledgeable; you need to have fresh knowledge in your field. You wouldn't want a doctor who promoted the 1990s version of the FDA food pyramid—eat tons of bread and grains and very few fruits and vegetables. That knowledge is out of date.

Uncommon achievers make themselves lifetime students in their field. If you're a preacher with a passion for things like cars or you love investing, consider quitting the ministry to do those things instead. Many people in the ministry should be doing something else, but they've allowed themselves to be pressured into the ministry. Maybe they were the only kid living for the Lord in their youth group. The youth pastor told them to go to Bible college, and they sort of fell into ministry, but their passion was never in ministry.

If I were sixteen years old and loved playing video games, I would look to make it a career. I would create my own YouTube or Twitch, and plan to make a living doing what I love. If I had a child who loved playing video games, I'd ask them if they'd started a YouTube channel, and if they hadn't, I'd tell them to start one or quit playing video games. Pay attention to what your child loves to do. You can make money doing anything.

Don't ignore your passion. What do you love to read about? What interests you? You don't have to get a normal job, although there's nothing wrong with having one. What would you love to do for fourteen hours straight? If you love to shop and could do it all day, then stop looking at it as a vice. You don't need to quit and settle for some job in a cubicle. You can make your own job—be a personal shopper. Millions of people hate shopping, but they enjoy having nice things.

If you love to golf, get good at it. If you love to fight, do it professionally, not illegally. Do you love working out? Choose a profession that has you in the gym all day—become a trainer. Many people treat their passion like a bad habit when it's actually their purpose.

We have a member of our church who's extremely warm and friendly. She loves talking to people. We hired her to call all our partners every month and pray with them. She loves doing it.

Can you imagine if Shaquille O'Neal's mother was more concerned with his reading skills than his basketball abilities? Find a way to make a living doing what you love—what you're naturally great at. There is a way, but it requires a creative solution. That's where God and His anointing come in. The Lord will show you what path to take to do what you love.

I don't thank my parents enough. My dad was and is an evangelist. If he wasn't an evangelist, I can only imagine how my parents might have responded to me traveling and preaching in my early twenties and coming home with three hundred bucks after driving fourteen hours round-trip. Their patience gave me the time I needed.

Tom Laipply's son, Charles, is an MMA fighter. While on the way to get something to eat late at night in Florida, Pastor Tom said, "I told Charles, 'You can live at home, and we'll take care of your bills until you're twenty-five years old. You have until then to make a run at MMA fighting.' He's in the gym four to six hours a day, and he's going for it. He knocked one opponent out in four seconds." Now, that is a great father.

For about six years after I finished Bible school, it looked like I was going nowhere. I made very little money. I used to preach at churches with less than thirty people, now I have double that amount any time I call a staff meeting. I know there are people with thousands of staff members, but for me, it's a big deal because it wasn't always like this.

Not too long ago, if my mom and dad would have sat me down and said, "Listen, this evangelism thing is not working out. You need to get serious and get a job," I wouldn't have been able to make a counterargument. There was nothing in my life that would have suggested I was going anywhere. That's why you don't make decisions based solely on what you see as your current circumstance. The Bible tells you not to despise the day of small beginnings, but that doesn't just mean for you; it also means for the people connected to you. Give people some runway; very few people take off at nineteen.

I follow comedians on social media because I like to laugh. Their stories are very similar to evangelist stories. Most started out performing standup comedy in clubs that paid twenty-five dollars or stiffed them altogether—I've had that happen to me too. They had to stay in some dump of a motel, but now they make $100,000 an appearance and fly on private jets. They didn't start that way, so don't despise the day of small beginnings.

SECRET 22

UNCOMMON ACHIEVERS HONOR THE LAW OF SIGHT

> Then the Lord took Abram outside and said to him, "Look up into the sky and count the stars if you can. That's how many descendants you will have!"
>
> — GENESIS 15:5

Uncommon achievers honor the law of sight. God gave Abram a picture, a visual representation of where he was headed. *Look up at the stars. That's where I'm taking you.*

Uncommon achievers look where they want to go, and God guided Abram to do just that. Ten years ago, I thought vision boards were silly, but I've listened to many great men and women talk about their vision boards, and now I recognize their significance. Dr. Pastor Paul Enenche built a church that seats 100,000 people. For a long time, their church was stuck at about 6,000. He was so determined to reach 20,000 that he wrote "20,000" on his bedroom ceiling. Every night as he lay down to sleep, it was the last thing he saw and the first thing he saw when he woke up. He wrote it on his bathroom door and by the mirror. The church crested 20,000 several years before he realized it because he looked at it for so long and got that vision in his spirit so strongly that when it happened, he wasn't even surprised.

 Where you're looking today will be where you live tomorrow.

Lot pitched his tents facing Sodom, and shortly afterward, he was living in Sodom (Genesis 13:12). Where you look today will be where you live tomorrow, and what you put in front of your eyes will affect your perception.

When I first considered buying a personal aircraft, I read a magazine Dr. Rodney Howard-Browne gave me from the fixed-base operator in Pittsburgh. A fixed-base operator (FBO) is a company that provides flight services at an airport for private aircraft and charter companies. The FBO's catalog listed all the jets a particular company had for sale. One had three guest bedrooms, two guest bathrooms, a master bedroom with a shower, a dining room, a living room, a theater, and a library. Suddenly, the ten-seat plane I was considering didn't seem like a big deal. Instead of feeling like I needed faith for something monumental, I felt like I was believing for a Honda Civic. If you think owning a private plane is a big deal, then it's a big deal. But when you start looking at jets that are basically flying mansions, you start to think, '*Well, if somebody can afford that, I can afford this.*'

Looking at something big expands your capacity. God showed Abram the stars to give him a picture. God promised to not only give him a son but also to give him descendants as numerous as the stars in the sky. There are over seven million Jewish people today, and that number is growing.

I follow an account on Instagram called *Robb Report*. They post pictures of extravagant yachts, homes, and hotels. I want to see what's out there because I want to see how great life is and how far you can go. When your capacity to see big things is expanded, you'll never be tricked into thinking something very attainable is out of reach.

It wasn't cheap for me to fly to Lagos, Nigeria, to visit Bishop David Oyedepo's church, but I needed to get a picture. I wanted to see what it was like to be in the largest church on planet Earth at the time. I wanted to see what 55,000 people at an indoor church service looked like, and I wanted to hear what a 5,000-person choir sounded like. I wanted to see 1,100 pastors in operation. Without that experience, I may have thought too highly of myself after our church reached one thousand members. When you've seen firsthand how far you can go, your perspective of where you are changes. You begin to see what's possible, and it expands your faith. When the Lord tells you that you'll have as many descendants as the stars in the sky, it gets easier to believe for one son. When Abram asked God for a son, He gave him seven million.

In John G. Lake's message titled *The Cry of the Soul*, he spoke about an office he liked in Chicago. He was a very wealthy man before he sold everything to preach in South Africa. Eventually, a building he acquired had the exact office he'd always wanted. God gave it to him without the need to build it himself. He believed when your heart is set on something, spiritual powers act on your behalf to create it for you. I could retell various stories of preachers and Christians who say that once they got a picture of what they wanted, it came into their hands.

Pastor Bob Nichols attended a Baptist church conference hosted in the most beautiful church he'd ever been to. "I said under my breath to the Lord in the lobby, 'It would be great for a Full Gospel church to have a building like this.'" Eleven or twelve years later, as that same church was closing, they called him to see if he was interested in making a deal to buy it. They felt he had the only church in the area capable of sustaining a building that size. The church he once visited and desired for Full Gospel work fell into his lap. He didn't receive a church like it; he received the exact same church. Don't tell me you don't create what you look at.

My dad shared similar stories about preaching in Alaskan villages. The first time he preached there, everyone wore traditional native attire. After the village was connected to the internet, he returned a year later to find all the kids in rural Alaska wearing backward Yankee hats and chains. What you look at replicates itself.

If you want to be an uncommon achiever, find out who the top person in your field is and visit them. Not at their home, that's creepy, but at their place of business or a conference. Being in the same space they operate in will expand your vision and your ability to realize what you see.

SECRET 23

UNCOMMON ACHIEVERS ADMIT WHEN THEY ARE WRONG

Uncommon achievers admit when they're wrong. So, don't hesitate to admit when you are wrong. If something is not working, shut it down. Don't run your life or your business into the ground because you're too proud to admit a mistake.

If I launched a ministry out of our church and after two years, we had spent $400,000, with no real value added, I could either keep hemorrhaging money without results or admit a mistake and shut it down. Maybe it wasn't implemented correctly, or God never called me to it, but I would shut it down. People start ventures that don't work out. I'm not suggesting you should quit at the first sign of hardship or opposition, but if it's been eleven years and you have nothing to show from it, re-examine your decision. Be humble enough to announce that you're changing directions.

Bishop David Oyedepo started a church that wouldn't grow. He couldn't get people to attend, and nothing worked. He prayed about it, and the Lord asked him, "Did I tell you to build that church?" Immediately after, he announced the closure of the church. His staff was worried. The building was there, and everyone knew he started the church. "Tough luck for me," he replied. "I bought a building that I'm not using. We'll do something else with it, but I won't keep something going just because I don't want to admit I'm wrong."

Uncommon achievers admit when they're wrong. Common underachievers can't do this because they pretend nothing ever goes wrong. I've followed several ministers on Instagram for a few years. Some have been through three wives, and I'm not exaggerating. Some never mentioned a divorce or separation; their wives just disappeared from their page. Others have started churches and shut them down without any announcement. They act like nothing happened. They're too proud to admit a mistake. If something doesn't go as planned, tell people. Tell people what you started isn't achieving the results you desired. Why hemorrhage money and waste years of your life on it? Shut it down and do something else instead.

Don't continue pursuing a failing endeavor for thirty-five years solely out of pride. Some people will go to Hell because they can't admit they're wrong. Their parents told them they were making a mistake by not serving the Lord, and they rebelled. Now, their life is in shambles, and they won't admit it. They refuse to attend church, and they won't get saved because if they did, it would mean admitting their mother was right all along. They'd rather go to Hell than admit they were wrong.

Pride comes before destruction. It prevents you from admitting when you're wrong. Some pastors won't go to Bishop David Oyedepo's church to see what he does because they'd have to admit he knows more than they do. They refuse to attend anyone else's conferences, and they won't listen to anyone else preach because they'd have to admit another preacher has something worth saying besides them. That's why *"pride comes before destruction and haughtiness before the fall"* (Proverbs 16:18). Admit your mistakes.

If I saw someone whose life was flourishing while my life was rotting, I would be humble enough to take note of what they were doing. It's good for family members to pray that God sends laborers into the field to reach their unsaved loved ones. Most often, people listen to a stranger over their family. You have to be humble enough to enjoy seeing your family member saved through someone else who told them everything you've already told them.

You don't have to make any mistakes, but if you do, admit it and move on. The sooner you make a correction, the better. It's never too late to be right. If I needed to travel on I-70 East and I accidentally took I-70 West, I wouldn't continue in the wrong direction until I ended up in Denver, Colorado, just to avoiding hearing, "See, I told you, we went the wrong way." Some people refuse to make a U-turn. If there's an area where you need to make a U-turn, make it today. Don't put it off for one single day.

Uncommon achievers have enough humility to admit when they're wrong. Pride brings destruction, and humility brings exaltation. *"Those who humble themselves will be exalted"* (Matthew 23:12). Humility causes you to re-examine your decisions. It allows you to learn from others and enables you to be an uncommon achiever.

SECRET 24

UNCOMMON ACHIEVERS REMAIN HUMBLE BY HONORING GOD AND HIS CHURCH

Jesus told him, "If you want to be perfect, go and sell all your possessions and give the money to the poor, and you will have treasure in heaven. Then come, follow me." But when the young man heard this, he went away sad, for he had many possessions. Then Jesus said to his disciples, "I tell you the truth, it is very hard for a rich person to enter the Kingdom of Heaven. I'll say it again—it is easier for a camel to go through the eye of a needle than for a rich person to enter the Kingdom of God!"

— MATTHEW 19:21-24

"Remember to observe the Sabbath day by keeping it holy. You have six days each week for your ordinary work, but the seventh day is a Sabbath day of rest dedicated to the Lord your God. On that day no one in your household may do any work. This includes you, your sons and daughters, your male and female servants, your livestock, and any foreigners living among you."

— EXODUS 20:8-10

Uncommon achievers remain humble by honoring God and His Church. If you're rich, this is a potential rebuke. If you're not wealthy yet, it's crucial to settle this in your spirit in advance. Rich people often think they're allowed to dictate their own set of rules. They think they don't have to go to church and don't plug into any church. Your concept of 'rich' depends on where you live. If you live in rural Arkansas and make over $100,000 a year—you're rich. If you live in Manhattan and you make over $100,000 a year, you're teetering on poverty. Regardless of your definition of rich, the fact is, as people get more money, more often than not, their church attendance drops.

God made the Earth in six days, and then He rested. The land is supposed to have a sabbath year of rest. If you violate God's principle of rest, you're in opposition to how God made the human body, and you'll die.

As God blesses you, you'll either become like Abraham and press into God more, or you'll be like most people who bounce in and out of churches. When you own a business, you grow accustomed to being in charge and doing all the talking. It can cause pride to develop in you and prevent you from listening to someone else speak. Some people can't attend a church if they are not on the board. Rich people often feel the need to announce their decision to attend a church and offer to sit on your board. Maybe you should sit and listen like everyone else, or would you prefer that everyone lay palm branches down on your way out of church so you don't have to walk on the pavement? Rich people frequently disappear from church for seasons at a time.

If your church attendance decreases as your income increases, I pray God would reduce your income to a level that allows you to stay faithful to Him. *"I tell you the truth, it is very hard for a rich person to enter the Kingdom of Heaven. I'll say it again—it is easier for a camel to go through the eye of a needle than for a rich person to enter the Kingdom of God!"* (Matthew 19:23-24). Jesus knew what He was talking about. Wealthy people often think themselves superior to their pastor and even higher than God. They believe they're doing their pastor a favor by attending church. It's the essence of pride.

I once watched my grandfather—who was a pastor—as a couple approached him after church and handed him a check for $10,000. As they handed him the check, they said, "There are some projects we would like to see this church complete, and we want to give this to enable you to do it." While still talking, my grandfather dropped the check on the floor and walked to his office. At fourteen years old, his reaction caused me to raise an eyebrow. I have a feeling he had been down that road before. He knew the spirit of pride caused those people to give, not a love for God and His house.

Pastor Rodney Howard-Browne has a funny saying, "There once was a man named Dave. The richer he got, the less he gave." It's not just about the giving; it's about a life with no regard for the church. If you make over $100,000 a year, how many "home churches" have you attended in the last ten years? If you've bounced around from church to church because you can't submit to authority, you have a pride issue.

Jesus told the rich young ruler to sell everything he owned, and because he was rich, he refused to listen to *Jesus*. I may not be the richest, but I am rich. Relative to the world standard, with the average person driving an oxcart, there's no question that I'm rich. Before I started this church, I was faithful to a church. When the church I attended shut down for COVID, I drove two hours to attend the only church open. I'm in church on vacation and every Sunday. You should have a home church. Don't bounce around. Having a church is not like attending revival meetings—you don't pick which one you want to go to. You should plant yourself in a church. One family in our church used to drive seven hours from Michigan to Pittsburgh to attend every Sunday service. Eventually, they bought a house nearby and moved. They left everything to live near the church that was spiritually feeding their entire family.

Everyone, including evangelists, needs a church, but most evangelists don't have a church home. Many have a church home in name only to receive financial support. They're not in it to receive from a pastor, let alone submit to one. My dad was an outstanding role model for me because, as an evangelist, whenever he was home on Sunday, he was in church. He sat two-thirds of the way toward the back and listened.

Many gospel music performers start in church, and when God blesses their music ministry, they go on tour with no further connection to a specific church or pastor. How many of them are still married to their first wife? How many of them watch as their entire lives collapse? *"In that day, I will give you shepherds; who watch over your souls"* (Jeremiah 3:15; Hebrews 13:7). If you get out from under that shepherd and become a "king sheep," thinking you can do whatever you want, you'll get in trouble. Uncommon achievers remain humble. Your church attendance is a sign of your humility, and your ability to sit and listen demonstrates your ability to give up control for a couple of hours. You have a serious control problem when you need to be in charge everywhere, including your church.

How many rich people start a home church—not have a home church, but start one? Money doesn't entitle you to start a church without any direction from God. Even so, the rich are not always to blame. Sometimes, it's pastors who approach the wealthiest members of their congregations and install them as associate pastors who teach and lead the church, even though they've never been called by God to ministry. They never attended Bible school. Most times, they don't have a spiritual bone in their body—just money in their pockets. They are people who did well in business and somehow have been entrusted to preach on Sundays. If a pastor doesn't teach sowing and reaping and doesn't sow himself, he will inevitably exalt rich people, just as James warned against. The Holy Ghost, through James, said not to exalt the rich, because He knew there was a tendency in human nature to do so (James 2:1-4).

You would never catch me in a church that operates out of someone's home. If a church starts out in someone's home, it better outgrow their house quickly. We're constantly outgrowing the places God blesses us with. How can a church meet in a living room for three years? That means no one is getting saved. I wish there were a way to calculate the percentage of home churches run by wealthy families that don't want to go to a church. I'm sure it's high. Biblical standards don't change because you have a business to run. Abraham, Solomon, and David ran entire nations and attended the Temple consistently. David prayed three times a day and praised God seven.

There is no excuse to be absent from church. It doesn't matter if you're poor and don't have a car, you're rich and own a large business, or you're middle class and are scheduled to work on Sundays. There is no excuse. The Devil doesn't have to convince you into believing people don't need a church—just that *you* don't. When you're no longer under a church covering, I guarantee your life will go south. Uncommon achievers remain humble by honoring God and His Church. The Church belongs to God, and when you honor the Church, you honor God.

Ask yourself these questions, especially if you're considered upper-middle class and beyond:

1. Where is your church home?
2. How many churches have you made your church home in the last ten years?
3. Does any pastor know you by name?

4. Are your children plugged into a children's ministry?
5. Have you made it impossible for your teenagers to plug into a youth ministry because you bounce around so often?

When God puts His hand on someone's life and empowers them to excel in business, it's a shame that kids often live sinful lives because they were never taught the source of their parent's success. Their family's resources gave them everything they wanted but not what they truly needed. If you refuse to submit and plant yourself in a home church, your kids will go to Hell, and it will be your fault.

> And the Lord said, Shall I hide from Abraham that thing which I do; Seeing that Abraham shall surely become a great and mighty nation, and all the nations of the earth shall be blessed in him? For I know him, that he will command his children and his household after him, and they shall keep the way of the Lord, to do justice and judgment; that the Lord may bring upon Abraham that which he hath spoken of him.
>
> — GENESIS 18:17-19 (KJV)

Put God first all the time, not just when your schedule is clear. Achieving worldly success while your own children end up in Hell is no success at all. There are rich businesspeople who consider themselves Christians and don't spend a single Sunday in church during the summer. You're not a pastor;

you're a businessman. You might make it to Heaven, but your poor prioritization will ensure that your children won't. There's not a huge difference between missing church to run your business on Sunday and skipping service to sit in a strip club. Either way, you disobeyed God. The only difference is the bait Satan used to draw you away from God. One is accepted by society, and the other isn't, but disobedience of any kind is unacceptable to God. Sadly, preachers and Christian leaders have less of a problem with the former, and they have more of a problem with the latter. I view them as equal because the result is still disobedience; the reason makes no difference. Maybe you think you're different or special. You have sneakers that cost nine hundred dollars and a belt with two Gs on it, so the rules don't apply to you. None of that makes you special. Be in church on Sunday.

A hundred years ago, Christians refused to compete in Olympic events if their competition fell on Sunday morning. That's the kind of commitment Christians used to have. When you believe you abide by a different set of rules because you have money, it's over. The commands of the Bible are not based on your income level.

Christians go to church on Sunday mornings. I didn't invent the concept. People are free to do it their way, but my way works because it's based on the Word and over 2,000 years of Christian history. It's not my interpretation. I follow what Christians did in 60 AD, 1600, and 1800—my path works, it's proven, and it's battle-tested.

SECRET 25

UNCOMMON ACHIEVERS UNDERSTAND THEIR BUSINESS IS A GOD-GIVEN MEANS TO CREATE WEALTH

"Be careful to obey all the commands I am giving you today. Then you will live and multiply, and you will enter and occupy the land the Lord swore to give your ancestors. Remember how the Lord your God led you through the wilderness for these forty years, humbling you and testing you to prove your character, and to find out whether or not you would obey his commands. Yes, he humbled you by letting you go hungry and then feeding you with manna, a food previously unknown to you and your ancestors. He did it to teach you that people do not live by bread alone; rather, we live by every word that comes from the mouth of the Lord. For all these forty years your clothes didn't wear out, and your feet didn't blister or swell. Think about it: Just as a parent disciplines a child, the Lord your God disciplines you for your own good. So obey the commands of the Lord your God by walking in his ways and fearing him. For the Lord your God is bringing you into a good land of flowing streams and pools of water, with fountains and springs that gush out in the valleys and hills. It is a land of wheat and barley; of grapevines, fig trees, and pomegranates; of olive oil and honey. It is a land where food is plentiful and nothing is lacking. It is a land where iron is as common as stone, and copper is abundant in the hills. When you have eaten your fill, be sure to praise the Lord your God for the good land he has given you. But that is the time to be careful! **Beware that in your plenty you do not forget the Lord your God and disobey his commands, regulations, and decrees that I am giving you today.**"

— DEUTERONOMY 8:1-11

Anti-prosperity people claim that if God blesses you, riches will take the place of God in your life, but it doesn't have to. The Bible warns us it's possible, not inevitable.

For when you have become full and prosperous and have built fine homes to live in, and when your flocks and herds have become very large and your silver and gold have multiplied along with everything else, **be careful!** Do not become proud at that time and forget the Lord your God, who rescued you from slavery in the land of Egypt. Do not forget that he led you through the great and terrifying wilderness with its poisonous snakes and scorpions, where it was so hot and dry. He gave you water from the rock! He fed you with manna in the wilderness, a food unknown to your ancestors. He did this to humble you and test you for your own good. He did all this so you would never say to yourself, 'I have achieved this wealth with my own strength and energy.' Remember the Lord your God. He is the one who gives you power to be successful, in order to fulfill the covenant he confirmed to your ancestors with an oath.

— DEUTERONOMY 8:12-18

The Amplified Classic translation says, *"It is He Who gives you power to get wealth"* (Deuteronomy 8:18). God needs a vessel to anoint, so He gave you the power to create wealth. If you own a business, its purpose is to create wealth. If you don't view your business as a tool to create wealth, it will never get off the ground. A business is a God-given vessel for creating wealth. God never vowed to stuff your mailbox full of money—He promised to bless the work of your hands. The work of your hand is the vessel God granted you to create wealth. Too often, Christians go into business and feel guilty about charging people. They feel that because they're a Christian, their business should bless people. Your business exists to create wealth.

Don't feel bad about charging people; make the most money possible—ethically and legally, of course. If a construction company wins the bid on a job for $40,000, and the next closest bid is $90,000, I guarantee they're not qualified. I told the contractors who worked to build out our church building that their families shouldn't have less so that I could get a deal. That's not good negotiating, but that's how I feel. I pay people more because I'm blessed. If you don't plant seeds, you'll never receive a harvest.

Some might say, "I want to offer free legal services to bless people." Think how many more people you could bless if you had a legal team that took in $90 million a year. Offering free services enables you to bless one family, but by charging appropriate retainers for your services, you can bless 10,000 families. If your goal is to bless people, look to create the most wealth possible. Step number one of being a philanthropist: Make a lot of money. You can't be a philanthropist without wealth.

The Dunkin Donuts by our old offices closed at 7:00 p.m. If I owned a coffee shop, it'd be open twenty-four hours. I would pay one person a reasonable hourly wage to work behind the counter for an extra eight hours. It might cost me an extra hundred dollars per day. But I would only need about $150 worth of sales throughout that eight-hour shift. In thirty or so coffees, the extra business hours paid for itself. I run a nonprofit, but I still know how to think aggressively.

Too often, the issue with Christian businesses is that they aren't diligent. They're lazy and slothful. God said to do the two opposite things: Be diligent in business, not slothful in business (Romans 12:11). I don't run a business. I run a ministry. We host a teaching program every day at 10:00 a.m., prayer every day at noon, and *Check the News* until almost midnight, and I don't do it to make a profit; I do it because I'm called to sow the Word. Everything I do in ministry, I do with all my might (Ecclesiastes 9:10). If you're going to do something, go after it!

God gave you one day to rest and six days to work. Start a side project on Saturdays. If you work a job from Monday through Friday, use all day Saturday to start a sixth-day project, as Pastor Willie George used to call it. Use Saturday to work on your dream while you work your job until that Saturday project overtakes your Monday through Friday employment. Go after it. Just because all the restaurants in your city are closed on Monday doesn't mean yours has to be. Sharpen your mind. Open before your competition. Stay open later than your competitors and outwork them.

The people who gave our church a building did it because they felt to do so. They didn't owe it to me. They had a right to ask whatever they wanted. If I didn't like the price, then I wouldn't have bought the building. If you're going to give, then give, but don't feel guilty for charging a premium and making a profit in business. Your time is worth it.

The Bible says labor not to be rich (Proverbs 23:4). That can be a confusing scripture. I don't labor to become rich; I preach to accrue wealth to feed the hungry, clothe the naked, build churches, and get the Gospel out. My motivation for going strong is to meet significant needs. As a Christian business owner, you should feel good about charging a premium price. Don't work for free because you'll never accumulate wealth. If you don't amass wealth, you can't be a blessing to the world. Earning $70,000 a year won't enable you to meet significant needs. You need to create a plan to go after much more so you can give much more because giving produces receiving.

I sent Jesse Duplantis $65,000, which was our church's tithe. That week was the second-greatest financial week our ministry has ever had. Within forty-eight hours, we received a check for almost a quarter-million dollars from someone who'd never given to our ministry. Then we received another check for $55,000 from a church I'd never preached in.

If you own a barbershop, charge seventeen dollars for a haircut, and are always booked solid, what's your next step? You might think it's time to hire, or maybe it's time to raise prices. You should actually do both.

 Supply and demand.

There's a barber in Boston who used to charge fifteen dollars for a haircut when he first started. But once word spread about the quality of his work, players from the Boston Celtics and the New England Patriots started coming to his shop. They spread the word to their friends in the NBA and the NFL, and now he cuts hair for prominent athletes and charges eighty dollars a haircut. When you have more requests for your services than you can respond to, it's time to increase your price. When word of your superiority spreads, charge more. People looking for a discount can hire another company. Higher prices connote higher quality. If you charge too little, it causes people to question your quality.

When a restaurant charges twenty dollars for a sushi roll, I assume it's superb sushi. Sushi for twelve dollars a roll is a reasonable price, but if a restaurant charges four dollars for a roll, I assume I'll die of a stomach ailment if I eat it. Some people don't want a deal; they prefer to tell people they paid a premium for a high-end product or service.

Uncommon achievers understand that their business is the vehicle God gifted them to make them wealthy. So go after it, and don't feel bad about charging people. Undercharging people is not a fruit of the Spirit. Christianity is not about doing things for free and causing your family to suffer so strangers get a better deal. That doesn't make any sense. You have a right to make a profit. Don't go back to that old way of thinking which keeps you poor.

 Never go back.

You'll never go back to Egypt. The God that brought you this far will keep taking you forward.

SECRET 26

UNCOMMON ACHIEVERS NAVIGATE FORWARD WHILE IN CRISIS

Three days later, when David and his men arrived home at their town of Ziklag, they found that the Amalekites had made a raid into the Negev and Ziklag; they had crushed Ziklag and burned it to the ground. They had carried off the women, children, and without killing anyone. When David and his men saw the ruins and realized what had happened to their families, they wept until they could weep no more. David's two wives, Ahinoam from Jezreel and Abigail, the widow of Nabal from Carmel, were among those captured. David was now in great danger because all his men were very bitter about losing their sons and daughters, and they began to talk of stoning him. But David found strength in the Lord his God. Then he said to Abiathar the priest, "Bring me the ephod!" So Abiathar brought it. Then David asked the Lord,

"Should I chase after this band of raiders? Will I catch them?" And the Lord told him, "Yes, go after them. You will surely recover everything that was taken from you!"

—1 SAMUEL 30:1-8

Uncommon achievers navigate forward while in crisis. Their life doesn't come to a grinding halt when they're faced with a difficult time. Unfortunately, most people go missing when they're hit with a hard time, but uncommon achievers pursue, overtake, and recover all.

 Pursue, overtake, and recover all.

You'll never know when an uncommon achiever is in a crisis because they don't walk around telling everyone. They don't post it on social media or publicly ask for prayer. If you need prayer, get it privately from someone who knows how to pray. I promise you, if you post it on Facebook, all the people who put praying hand emojis will never actually pray.

David encouraged himself in the Lord. He drew closer to God, not farther away like many people do when they're going through a rough time. David called for the priest, entered into the presence of God, and drew strength to move forward.

SECRET 27

UNCOMMON ACHIEVERS DON'T ALLOW OTHERS' CRISES TO DETERMINE THEIR ACTIONS

A man named Lazarus was sick. He lived in Bethany with his sisters, Mary and Martha. This is the Mary who later poured the expensive perfume on the Lord's feet and wiped them with her hair. Her brother, Lazarus, was sick. So the two sisters sent a message to Jesus telling him, "Lord, your dear friend is very sick." But when Jesus heard about it he said, "Lazarus's sickness will not end in death. No, it happened for the glory of God so that the Son of God will receive glory from this." So although Jesus loved Martha, Mary, and Lazarus, he stayed where he was for the next two days. Finally, he said to his disciples, "Let's go back to Judea." But his disciples objected. "Rabbi," they said, "only a few days ago the people in Judea were trying to stone you. Are you going there again?" Jesus replied, "There are twelve hours of daylight every day. During the day people can walk safely. They can see because they have the light of this world. But at night there is danger of stumbling because they have no light." Then he said, "Our friend Lazarus has fallen asleep, but now I will go and wake him up." The disciples said, "Lord, if he is sleeping, he will soon get better!" They thought Jesus meant Lazarus was simply sleeping, but Jesus meant Lazarus had died. So he told them plainly, "Lazarus is dead. And for your sakes, I'm glad I wasn't there, for now you will really believe. Come, let's go see him." Thomas, nicknamed the Twin, said to his fellow disciples, "Let's go, too—and die with Jesus." When Jesus arrived at Bethany, he was told that Lazarus had already been in his grave for four days. Bethany was only a few miles down the road from Jerusalem, and many of the people had come to console Martha and Mary in their loss. When Martha got word that Jesus was coming, she went to meet him. But Mary stayed in the house. Martha said to Jesus, "Lord, if only you had been here, my brother would not have died."

— JOHN 11:1-21

When they tried to rush Jesus, He responded, "I only do what I see the Father do. I only say what I see the Father say." No one could deter Him from doing exactly that. Someone else's problem doesn't have to become your emergency. What's of dire importance to others doesn't need to be important to you. I would never teach if I allowed other people's problems to dictate my words. People will try to pull you off track, but uncommon achievers don't allow other people's crises to determine their actions.

There's no greater example of this than Jesus with Lazarus. Lazarus was his friend. Imagine if you were the son of God, a miracle worker capable of walking on water, and someone you love is sick and dying. People would expect you to be there. Jesus wasn't even preaching; he was chilling. There's no record in John 11 of Jesus performing any ministry tasks.

If you're not careful, you'll become a slave to what people think you should do. I know people in their fifties who still allow their mothers to control their lives. When you're a pastor, everyone you speak to thinks their issue is of the utmost importance, and they want it to be important to you, too. But as Peter said, we can't run a feeding program. Pastors are given to the ministry of the Word and prayer. It's not that you want to be a jerk, but you have to do what's best. How other people feel about it is their problem.

This is the only place you read where Jesus got somewhere, and the people weren't fawning over him. You can sense Lazarus' sister was upset. Her first words weren't welcoming. *"Lord, if only you had been here, my brother would not have died."*

I sleep with my phone on "do not disturb." I take it off "do not disturb" when I'm ready to start my day. If I have things to do in the morning, I leave it on "do not disturb." I won't let somebody's panicked phone call dictate my actions.

SECRET 28

UNCOMMON ACHIEVERS ARE IMMUNE TO THE OPINIONS OF OTHERS

> Now when he was in Jerusalem at the passover, in the feast day, many believed in his name, when they saw the miracles which he did. But Jesus did not commit himself unto them, because he knew all men, And needed not that any should testify of man: for he knew what was in man.
>
> — JOHN 2:23-25 (KJV)

Uncommon achievers are immune to the opinions of others—good or bad. The Bible doesn't say the people insulted Jesus. They believed Him. They thought he was great. But He knew before long they'd want Him dead and a murderer released in His place. Don't allow compliments or insults to move you. They should both mean the same to you —which is not much.

> Speak not in the ears of a fool: for he will despise the wisdom of thy words.
>
> — PROVERBS 23:9 (KJV)

It's not what men say about you that matters in life; it's what you believe about yourself that matters (Proverbs 23:7). When someone writes a critical comment, I'm sure they think I'm half out of my mind. When I'm asked questions like, "How could you fly in a private jet when people are starving?" I usually reply, "I paid for it with your mother's money." Proverbs 23:9 says not to answer a fool.

 Never take time to explain yourself to someone who's committed to misunderstanding you.

If somebody desires to be taught, I'll teach them everything I know. If you don't control the part of you that reacts to people's opinions, you'll end up on a lot of medication for your mind and body. You'll be out of commission for three days every time the Devil sends one person to your comment section.

Montreal is not the most receptive city to preach the prosperity message. Before I really believed in prosperity, I mentioned from the pulpit that someone brought me to a warehouse with nice Italian suits and told me to pick out any three for myself. Later, someone ripped me to shreds in the comments on Facebook. They called me a false prophet—a wolf in sheep's clothing—and claimed all I did was talk about my nice suits for fifteen minutes. I was poised to respond when I felt the Lord speak to me. "If this guy can take up forty-five minutes of your time, I'll keep you small for your own sake because as you grow, bigger people will take shots at you—not some anonymous Facebook person." The Lord continued: "You haven't spoken to Adalis in the last forty-five minutes." Adalis had said something, and I responded, "Hold on a second," while I thought of a clever response to defend myself. He continued, "It's pulled you away from your wife and daughter for forty-five minutes. What will you do when there are one hundred comments? Will you go in a room and go to war with people on Facebook?" Then, I felt the Lord tell me to check how many followers he had. He had one follower. His profile picture was a wolf with green eyes. Who cares?

One of Pastor Rodney Howard-Browne's favorite sayings is, "Opinions are like armpits. Everyone has them, and some of them stink." Opinions don't matter. It doesn't matter whether opinions are positive or negative. It's nice to hear refreshing things, but don't allow them to hold any weight. A lady once told me I was the best evangelist she'd ever heard, but when I asked her who else she'd heard, she admitted I was the only one. It's like being named the valedictorian of your home-schooled class. Don't allow compliments to inflate your ego or let insults put you in the fetal position for three days.

If you read a negative comment about yourself or your business, and it bothered you so much that you become short-tempered with your wife, you're allowing opinions to affect things that actually matter. Why would anyone give a stranger that kind of space in their life? Don't waste your energy on a fool. Just skip it.

 You must have a gatekeeping system.

Have a gatekeeping system. If you're the head of a business or ministry, you shouldn't be answering random phone calls. People shouldn't be able to reach you whenever they want. During COVID, we received over four hundred death threats after the decision to keep our ministry open. I didn't see a single one of them. Magalis, Revival Today's head of administration, saw them. Only good news and testimonies make their way to me. I'm made aware of stories that lift me up. Have the gatekeepers destroy the bad news. I will not devote time in the pulpit to defending myself.

Not everything demands a response. The old saying is, if you don't want to offend people, don't get out of bed in the morning, and then you'll inevitably offend someone for not getting out of bed. As long as you live, people will be offended; this has never been truer than it is now.

Don't over-apologize. If an apology needs to be made, do it in person. Never apologize to a group of people on social media. If I were to say something out of line about an individual, I would apologize to them directly, not issue a mass public apology to groups of people whose sole purpose is to be offended. Most people aren't interested in resolutions; they're out to kill you because they don't like you. You'll never appease them. You'll sacrifice vital productivity, wasting your time trying to put out fires fueled by emotions. Half of the time, people who take offense simply suffer from low blood sugar and need a snack. Some ice cream and a nap are the cure for their hurt feelings. Don't pander to people. You'll waste your life.

SECRET 29

UNCOMMON ACHIEVERS REFUSE TO HAVE GRASSHOPPER COMPLEX

> "The land we traveled through and explored will devour anyone who goes to live there. All the people we saw were huge. We even saw giants there, the descendants of Anak. Next to them we felt like grasshoppers, and that's what they thought, too!"
>
> — NUMBERS 13:32-33

Uncommon achievers refuse to have Grasshopper Complex. The reason the ten spies were unable to take the Promised Land had nothing to do with how they viewed God. They never said one negative thing about God. They never claimed God wasn't mighty enough to give them the land. Every negative word they uttered was about themselves. Thousands of years later, the ten spies were obviously wrong about their opinion of their enemies. The Bible says their hearts were melting within them, even though their reality was the opposite of what they feared. You can become so delusional about your situation that your fear determines the outcome of your life. God had promised the land to the Israelites, but because the spies saw themselves as grasshoppers, they were unable to obtain what God promised them, and their greatest fear came upon them and their children. Their only punishment was that they received exactly what they said.

> Then the Lord said to Moses and Aaron, "How long must I put up with this wicked community and its complaints about me? Yes, I have heard the complaints the Israelites are making against me. Now tell them this: 'As surely as I live, declares the Lord, I will do to you the very things I heard you say.'"
>
> — NUMBERS 14:26-28

How you view and refer to yourself determines your destiny. The spies never mentioned God. They never mention God's abilities in their report. Their wicked report was centered on what they thought about themselves. They felt like grasshoppers. They disregarded God and His opinion, and that decision brought about their demise. People continue to do the same thing today. They disregard the Word and discredit God and His instructions. It's why they continue moving in circles, stuck in the same mess, frustrated because they refuse to see what the Word of God says about them.

The Bible is a mirror. Anyone who reads it, walks away, and forgets what they look like is crazy—they miss the whole point (James 1:22-25). The Word of God was written to enable us to glance into this mirror and clearly see what needs to be removed. You can't be filled with insecurity and fulfill the call of God on your life. It's not by your power that you fulfill your purpose—it's by God's Spirit (Zechariah 4:6-7). When you rest in the knowledge that His Spirit leads you, everything becomes ridiculously easy.

You'll never accomplish anything with a grasshopper complex. If you see yourself as weak and small, other people will too.

Do you want to write a book? Don't allow the fact that other books have already been written on your topic. If you want to write a book about motherhood, write one. Don't worry about who has done it before you.

I wanted to write a book on marriage, so after thirteen years of marriage, Adalis and I wrote one together. Do you want me to wait until I'm seventy-five years old and most of my friends are dead and can't buy the book? People need help in their marriages right now. I can use my perspective as a husband of thirteen years to help others. I'm sure much better books have been published than the one we wrote on marriage, but we didn't let the grasshopper complex stop us.

No matter what you purpose to do, someone has already done it, or done it better than you. This mindset deterred me from writing books on faith, healing, or prosperity for a long time because I felt what already existed was better than what I could write. T. L. Osborn's book, *Healing the Sick*, is way better than my books on healing, *Dominion Over Sickness and Disease*, and *How God Heals without Doctors, Medicine, or Surgery*. But I discovered that those impacted by my ministry wanted to know my belief on healing, not what T. L. Osborn believed. So, I wrote a book that did just that.

Your life is not determined by what God says about you or what people say about you—your life will be determined by what you believe about yourself.

> "For assuredly, I say to you, whoever says to this mountain, 'Be removed and be cast into the sea,' and does not doubt in his heart, but believes that those things he says will be done, he will have whatever he says."
>
> — MARK 11:23 (NKJV)

> **He who believes that the things that He says will be done will have what He says.**

Brother Kenneth Hagin called this principle "having faith in your faith," and the religious world flipped out at the thought. If you don't have faith that your prayers, words, and steps work, and if you don't have faith that your steps are ordered by the Lord, then you'll never truly walk by faith. Faith is not believing in God and His Word alone. Jesus said we must believe that the things we say will come to pass. You must believe that what you say will come to pass. Faith is voice-activated. You must release the Word out of your mouth. Your mindset needs to be, 'I declared it, that means it's done,' not, 'Well, I prayed, but it's up to God.' Part of the recipe of faith is believing that what *you* say will come to pass.

Uncommon achievers do not allow themselves to have a grasshopper complex. You are a child of God, and you're anointed to accomplish what God has called you to do. All things that pertain to life and godliness have been delivered to you.

SECRET 30

UNCOMMON ACHIEVERS HAVE ETHICS AND FOLLOW THE LAW

> Then the presidents and princes sought to find occasion against Daniel concerning the kingdom; but they could find none occasion nor fault; forasmuch as he was faithful, neither was there any error or fault found in him.
>
> — DANIEL 6:4 (KJV)

Uncommon achievers have personal ethics and follow the law. Before they made a law against prayer, the Bible says in Daniel 6:4 that the rulers sought to find any instance of Daniel breaking the law. When you succeed, and you will, your finances will come under attack. During COVID, we hired a lawyer to oppose the attorney general of Pennsylvania so we could hold our Easter service. As a religious organization, the only way the state can attack is to investigate whether we paid unemployment tax and reported it correctly. After standing against wickedness, our unemployment tax records were audited for the first time in our ministry's history. We had everything in order, but if I had cut corners, I would have had a problem. Your life needs to be guarded against attack. Most people will encourage you to cut corners, especially on taxes. When your business or ministry is small, no one cares. No one comes after your income taxes if you make under $42,000 a year. If you made a mistake, they might get an extra eight hundred dollars from you. It's not worth the effort. But if you make $42 million a year and they find something wrong, they're entitled to a multi-million-dollar payday. If your ministry upsets wicked powers, it's not just about money for them—they'll do everything in their power to take you out.

In Pakistan, if you ruffle the wrong feathers, they kill you. In America, they ruin your life, seize your bank accounts, and put you in federal prison. That's the goal of the wicked. Keeping that in mind, you must begin to think, 'If I was the Devil, how would I come after me?' Then put a buffer in every one of those areas. Build buffers to separate you from problems. When you become successful, people will come after you. I have people with me in the office everywhere I go. Everything is on camera.

Uncommon achievers have personal ethics and follow the law. If you live in America, you don't have to follow unconstitutional laws or edicts that are immoral or against God's laws. There are illegal laws like the ones they tried to pass during COVID. You don't follow laws that make you deny your faith. Adolf Hitler never did anything illegal; he passed his own laws.

When they told Daniel he couldn't pray, he refused to obey. They had to pass special laws to take him down because Daniel played by the book in every other way.

I know people who, when invited to preach in another country, told the border patrol they were visiting a family member. They hid their ministry products in a suitcase to avoid taxes. You can operate that way when you have a small ministry, but not when you're a televised minister who's advertised crusade at the Air Canada Center, and the border patrol agents have seen your billboards. When you're asked to state your purpose in Canada, border patrol already knows the reason for your visit.

If you can't play straight, God might keep you small for your own good. If you operate fast and loose when you're small and continue to do so as you grow, you'll end up in jail. For many, the only reason they aren't in jail right now is simply because they're too small for anyone to care. God will keep them small for their own safety, to keep them out of jail and from ruining themselves.

 You don't grow big, then manage well— you manage well to grow big.

Before Jesus multiplied the fish and bread, He instructed everyone to sit in groups of one hundred so that nothing was wasted. Jesus first established order. Too many people expect God to release the blessing because they want to be blessed, but if there's no action plan, your blessing will be inhibited.

I've instructed Patrick to maintain our finances as if an FBI agent had been assigned to inspect all our finances. I told him I didn't want any gray areas. Document everything. After an offering, some ministers grab a fist full of cash and take their guests out to lunch, but that's illegal. Choosing not to follow laws and ethics will land you in prison. When I travel to another country, I don't say I'm coming to teach; I tell them I'm coming to preach. If they don't want preachers, I'll go home. I'm not interested in lying and sneaking around. God will open the door if He wants me there. I won't force anything. If the Lord is in it, I don't need to jump through hoops to preach in another country. If the Lord wants me to be somewhere, He'll make a way for me to be there. I don't need help from a foreign government, and neither will I inject anything into my body to preach in another country. If you don't have standards, the ends will always justify the means.

SECRET 31

UNCOMMON ACHIEVERS ACCEPT THE LIFE OF A RICH MAN AND THE PERSECUTION THAT COMES WITH IT

Peter started to say to Him, Behold, we have yielded up and abandoned everything [once and for all and joined You as Your disciples, siding with Your party] and accompanied You [walking the same road that You walk]. Jesus said, Truly I tell you, there is no one who has given up and left house or brothers or sisters or mother or father or children or lands for My sake and for the Gospel's who will not receive a hundred times as much now in this time—houses and brothers and sisters and mothers and children and lands, with persecutions—and in the age to come, eternal life.

— MARK 10:28-30 (AMPC)

Uncommon achievers accept the life of a rich man and the persecution that comes with it. If you are willing and obedient, you'll eat the good of the land (Isaiah 1:19). Many are obedient, but they're not willing. They might be willing to obey what God said in the Bible but not to put up with the persecution that God's blessing brings. When God blesses you, people will hate you for it. Ask Joseph what happens when your dad gives you a coat of many colors; your own brothers conspire to kill you. You either come to grips with this fact or live a conflicted life. Subconsciously, you limit your growth to avoid the squint-eye scrutiny from others.

Jesus said you'll receive a hundredfold—property, lands, and houses, but He also said it comes with persecution. Jesse Duplantis has a beautiful aircraft, and he's taken a lot of heat for it. Likewise, Kenneth Copeland has endured the same. Joel Osteen hasn't taken a salary from his church since the early 2000s, but people still criticize him for living in a large home. It shouldn't be difficult to comprehend that someone who's written over a dozen N.Y. Times Bestselling books lives in a nice home. Jesus' life is an example of how you can do everything right, and people still want to kill you. Once you come to grips with that, you won't subconsciously limit your success by bending to the fear of persecution.

A friend in the ministry bought a Cadillac Escalade when he was close to fifty years old. Not too long after, he sold it and never bought another one because he wanted to avoid the judgmental looks he received from pastors when he pulled up to their churches. In reality, it highlights what's possible with

God. It should inspire pastors. If people resent your blessing, they're the ones with the problem.

I'm happy to see people doing well, whether they're in my faith or not. I'm glad when people aren't struggling. I don't want people to go hungry and live under constant pressure. I'm glad to see families doing well. I don't wish ill on people, let alone one of my brothers or sisters in Christ. Anyone who resents someone else's blessing has a real problem.

As soon as you become the top achiever, others will turn against you. This is your fair warning. Jesus said you'd receive one hundredfold return and one hundredfold persecution, so be prepared to deal with it. If you try to hide your blessing, it will make matters worse. You know the old saying: "The cover-up is worse than the crime."

That's why I live my life in a way that makes it impossible for me to be exposed. I post a picture of a plane whenever I fly. I share it to inspire people. I don't hide anything. I want my partners to know how I travel. If you think I should drive through the night to get from Cincinnati back to Pittsburgh and arrive an hour before church Sunday morning, having slept in my same clothes, then you should partner with another ministry. That's not how I operate. I'm very clear about how I operate. I don't hide anything, and I sleep like a baby at night.

You don't have to be a jerk about it, but don't hide it, either. Don't use what you have to condemn people; use it to inspire people. Some family members won't like that you're rich. Some Christians won't like it either, and the media surely won't like it. Remember, the world takes no issue with a child-molesting billionaire in the flow of the anti-Christ spirit, but if you're fulfilling your righteous, God-given assignment, you're only allowed a fraction of the money. I'm glad I'm rich. I'm glad I'm blessed, and I'm not ashamed of it. If someone else has a problem with it, I wish them all the best. I refuse to live at a lower standard to accommodate petty people. The people who don't like that Jesse Duplantis has a plane would also be upset if he had a bicycle. The truth is, they wish he were dead. They're upset he's a preacher. They don't like that the Gospel is being preached. He couldn't have little enough to make those types of people happy because it's a demon spirit driving them to anger (Ephesians 6:12).

SECRET 32

UNCOMMON ACHIEVERS MOVE QUICKLY

Now [in Haran] the Lord said to Abram, Go for yourself [for your own advantage] away from your country, from your relatives and your father's house, to the land that I will show you. And I will make of you a great nation, and I will bless you [with abundant increase of favors] and make your name famous and distinguished, and you will be a blessing [dispensing good to others]. And I will bless those who bless you [who confer prosperity or happiness upon you] and curse him who curses or uses insolent language toward you; in you will all the families and kindred of the earth be blessed [and by you they will bless themselves]. So Abram departed, as the Lord had directed him.

— GENESIS 12:1-4 (AMPC)

Uncommon achievers move quickly. The opportunity of a lifetime must be seized within the lifetime of the opportunity. If you wait, you'll miss it. You'll make more mistakes by being careful than you will by moving quickly. Make your mistakes moving fast and forward. Don't miss your chance to carry out God's instructions by dragging your feet. Whenever God spoke to Abraham, he moved immediately. Anytime God gave him an instruction, it was carried out the same day. The only exception was when God told him to sacrifice Isaac, the Bible says, "early the next morning." One time, Abraham waited one day. How long have you waited to move on God's instruction?

Move fast. Run hard. Don't hang around people who take sabbaticals. You don't need to rest; you need to work, especially when you're between the ages of twenty and sixty years old. Those are your production years. Lester Sumrall said, "A man's life can be broken into three segments: zero to thirty, your learning years; thirty to sixty, your production years; and sixty to ninety, your replication years." From zero to thirty, God puts people in your life to teach you. You'll never stop learning, but those formative years are the main thrust of your life. You don't stop learning in the next phase. It's also not to suggest that you don't produce anything from zero to thirty years of age, but during that time, God will place people around you to learn from. It's a time when you might attend Bible school or enroll in business school.

Thirty to sixty are your production years. It's the time to produce, not take vacations once a month. If you do well during your production years, by the time you reach sixty, opportunities to replicate yourself in others will begin to manifest.

At sixty, I'll probably speak at Bible colleges more than I host crusades. I will have created a platform impactful enough that people will want to know the how behind the what. It will be a time to replicate myself in a younger generation.

When I met Evangelist Dag Heward-Mills, I asked him, "Knowing what you know now, what would you do differently at my age?" He told me he wouldn't do anything differently. Then he shared that his secret has always been to move quickly. Every time a door opened, he busted through it. When the door opened for us to hold outdoor crusades, it looked like it would bankrupt our ministry. I'd rather go bankrupt and realize I was incapable of carrying out what God called me to do than sit on a porch at seventy-five years old and wonder how life would've turned out if I had given it my all. I went for it, and I never went bankrupt or hit bottom—everything went straight up from there.

In 2 Kings 7, four lepers had the chance to find food in a famine or stay where they were and die. Lepers were considered unclean according to Jewish law, and their condition was contagious, so they were banished to live outside the city.

The lepers said, *"Why should we sit here waiting to die?"* they asked each other. *"We will starve if we stay here, but with the famine in the city, we will starve if we go back there. So we might as well go out and surrender to the Aramean army. If they let us live, so much the better. But if they kill us, we would have died anyway"* (2 Kings 7:3-4). Instead of looking at their condition, the lepers chose to do the unthinkable. They left the city in search of food from the Syrian army fighting against Israel, and what happened after that decision was incredible. The Bible says God caused the Syrian army to hear a sound like chariots. They thought Israel had sent out their neighboring enemies, the Egyptians and Hittites, to attack them, so they ran away at night, and by morning, all the spoils of war (food included) were left at the disposal of the lepers and Israel. Needless to say, the lepers did not die, but instead, they ended up winning big-time, saving themselves and the nation of Israel.

Similarly, Queen Esther faced a life or death situation: the life or death of all the Jews in Persia who were at the mercy of her husband, King Xerxes. She heard Haman, the king's evil second-in-command, had masterminded a plot to wipe out the Jews in a mass execution that the king unknowingly approved. She was unable to alert him because of a law that he had to formally summon someone to hear their case. If you broke this law and tried to speak to him without a meeting, you would die. She said, *"If I must die, I must die"* (Esther 4:16). She summoned the Jews to fast with her for three days, went straight to the king, and saved herself and her people.

You must have the same attitude as the lepers and Esther did. Your life is on the line. Moving on what God tells you to do is a life and death situation, but when God sends you out and you obey Him, you can't lose. I promise your situation may not be as dramatic as Esther's or the lepers', and even if it is, you must take that leap of faith and move quickly because something great is at stake on the other side of your decision to act.

It is said that ninety-five percent of the things we fear never happen, and God commands us not to fear (1 John 4:18), so you have nothing to lose when you move quickly on what you know God has called you to do.

Our first building was given to us, but only after the previous owner saw how quickly we moved to get the building ready to hold services. I had no idea why he decided to give us the building until one night after *Check the News*, I came outside to find him waiting for me. He wanted me to know the reason he gave me the building was because of how quickly we moved on it. When he told me we could start working on it, the next day, Abel showed up with a team to begin building it out. He told me if I hadn't done that, he would've never given us the building. Our speed made him want to give it to us.

If most people were given a building, it would sit empty while they attempted to raise enough money. Things don't work the way most people think. You might assume it's wise to appeal to a successful person by approaching them like a desperately needy charity. It's the mindset of most churchgoers and ministry leaders. They believe if they portray themselves as poor and in need, they'll tug on people's emotions. They believe that presenting a woe-is-me mentality motivates people, but that's not how it works. Success and production attract success and output. Unfortunately, most Christians present the opposite of success; they present their need, lack, and stress. That attitude won't invoke anyone to sow or believe in their vision. It just doesn't work that way. Instead of focusing on survival and merely maintaining the present, set your sights on overwhelming production. Talk to people about what you plan to achieve ten years into the future.

People may give trinkets to help your needs, but they invest in productivity. If you appeal to people like you're in need, then people will give you what they would give to needy people—hats, socks, gloves, and ramen. But if you speak to them about production and success, people will invest.

SECRET 33

UNCOMMON ACHIEVERS ARE EXCELLENT

> Whatever may be your task, work at it heartily (from the soul), as [something done] for the Lord and not for men.
>
> — COLOSSIANS 3:23 (AMPC)

Uncommon achievers are excellent. Everything you do should be done as unto the Lord. Excellence attracts excellence. Some preachers can pull large crowds, but they're broke because no one is interested in giving a $250,000 check to a guy who looks like he just did three lines of coke in a Dave & Buster's bathroom. I've attended churches where I would never have handed a $10,000 check to their ushers because every one of them looked like he would have run off with it. Excellence produces and attracts excellence. You should look excellent.

There was a time when even poor people used to dress to the nines for church. If you look at old photos of baseball games from the 1920s, all the men wore suits and ties. There are photographs of men in breadlines during the Great Depression who dressed better than many business executives do today. There's an un-excellent spirit in many people today, and it's shameful.

When Ryan Seacrest hosted American Idol, he wore a well-groomed suit and tie even though the show's target demographic was eighteen to thirty-five. He didn't wear a Jerome Bettis jersey and some ripped jeans; he wore a designer suit and tie.

The number one program on Christian television features Joel Osteen. He wears a suit and tie. If you think you need to be casual to reach people, you need to rethink. It's mostly charismatic churches where people dress like bums to reach people. It's shameful. The expression *Sunday best* originated as a description of how people dressed to attend church. They wore their nicest outfit because they were meeting with the Lord at His house. That's all but gone now. Don't let that attitude leave you; bring it back in style! There should be an excellent standard in your dress, your home, and your vehicle. It's not your car that makes you poor; your care for your car makes you poor. It's not your clothes that make you raggedy; it's the care you have for your clothes that makes you look that way.

When my grandfather pastored, he would ensure the church lawn was cut on Saturday night, so it was fresh for Sunday morning. One time, someone made the mistake of cutting it on Friday. I was in the office when my grandfather laid into the landscaper, "What part of Saturday evening did you not understand?" Another thing my grandfather did that I decided to implement was that he always took his shoes to be shined. I want cleaned and shined shoes for my Sunday best. Don't dress for where you are; dress for where you're going.

> Then Pharaoh sent and called Joseph, and they brought him hastily out of the dungeon: and he shaved himself, and changed his raiment, and came in unto Pharaoh.
>
> — GENESIS 41:14 (KJV)

For a long time, I thought either Pharaoh or one of his officials made Joseph shave, change clothes, and shower when he was taken from prison, but that's not the case. Joseph made a point to present himself to Pharaoh in a respectable manner because he knew if he looked like a prisoner, he'd stay in prison. People treat you based on to how you look. It isn't fair, but that's life. God told us man judges by outward appearance (1 Samuel 16:7). You can either let it work against you, or you can make it work for you.

SECRET 34

UNCOMMON ACHIEVERS EMBRACE THEIR UNIQUE SKILL SET AND RARE TALENT STACK

Uncommon achievers embrace their unique skill set and rare talent stack. David had many talents that don't traditionally work together. He was an accomplished musician, songwriter, and a great fighter. Imagine if, after winning, a UFC fighter took out a harp during the interview and began playing. These are talents you might assume a person would be better off picking one or the other, but God gave them to the same person.

You don't have to choose between your talents. Embrace them and learn how to blend them, as David did. Don't allow people to tell you how to use the talents God has given you. That's what Saul tried to do when he gave David his sword and armor.

Jimmy Swaggart was the first person to play the piano, sing, and then preach. Until he came along, you were either a musician or a preacher. Jimmy Swaggart embraced his unique talent stack. He'd sit at the piano before he preached, telling stories about his life and singing. By the time he was ready to preach, everyone was crying from the anointing on the music. As he transitioned to the message, he had their full attention.

I like to make people laugh, I like to insult people, and I like to preach. I found a way to put them all together. That's how *Check the News* was birthed. I always had a side of me that no one except those closest to me knew. Then I discovered a platform that allowed me to combine all aspects of who I am. You might not like my style, but there's no one else like me. There was nobody else like David, there was nobody else like Jimmy Swaggart, and there's nobody like you.

Religion will insist that you exchange your slingshot for Saul's armor, but you don't have to listen. Embrace your unique talent stack. Otherwise, you'll make yourself replaceable and unremarkable. You'll be commonplace if your church or business blends in with everything else, but when you embrace your unique talent stack and lean into the unique person God created you to be, there's nobody like you.

If you're not careful, religious tradition or business training will turn you into someone who can be replaced at any time. You must find the platform that allows you to use your full stack. Jeff Ross was a decent comedian until he discovered stand-up comedy wasn't his best talent. His unique gift in comedy is roasting people, earning him the nickname "The Roastmaster General." Now, he's recognized as one of the best. Artie Lange wasn't a top-level comic until he became the second chair on *The Howard Stern Show*—that was where he shined. Find the platform that showcases your unique talent stack.

Some people suck at preaching, but they have a great podcast. Some people are terrible podcasters, but they're great at preaching. Find the forum that draws out the best in you. What brings creativity out of you? What are two or three things you do with excellence? How can you group them to create something uniquely you?

There was nothing like *Check the News* in existence before we made it. There was no reference point, but it's how I express myself best. Find a way to express yourself that comes naturally to you, otherwise, you're just copying other people.

SECRET 35

UNCOMMON ACHIEVERS RUN HARD

I must work the works of Him who sent Me while it is day; the night is coming when no one can work.

— JOHN 9:4 (NKJV)

Uncommon achievers run hard. Look at what Jesus did in three and a half years. Too many people plan their lives as if we still have Old Testament lifespans. I hear people in their sixties talk about what they're thinking about doing. At that age, you might want to quit thinking and start doing. We don't live into our six-hundreds anymore. Get moving. It's time to start moving on whatever is in your heart. Don't wait until you're fifty.

Jesus said, *"We must all quickly carry out the tasks assigned to us by the Father, for night comes when no man can work"* (John 9:4). The faster you move in the assignment God gave you, the more you'll see

His hand come behind you to help bring it to pass. God enjoys people who move quickly. Evangelist Reinhard Bonnke said, "God runs with the runners; he doesn't sit with the sitters." Don't claim you're waiting on God—God is not slow. Get moving, and watch God move with you.

What is on your heart to do? Why do you think it will be easier to do in three years than it is right now? Get moving today. Today, you are the oldest you've ever been. It's time to run hard, work quickly, and stop being careful. The Bible says to *"be careful for nothing"* (Philippians 4:6).

SECRET 36

UNCOMMON ACHIEVERS CONFRONT SIN

Then the Lord said to Samuel: "Behold, I will do something in Israel at which both ears of everyone who hears it will tingle. In that day I will perform against Eli all that I have spoken concerning his house, from beginning to end. For I have told him that I will judge his house forever for the iniquity which he knows, because his sons made themselves vile, and he did not restrain them.

— 1 SAMUEL 3:11-13 (NKJV)

Uncommon achievers confront sin. What you don't confront, you'll never conquer. What you don't resist has a right to remain. What you don't stand against will destroy you.

A pastor decided to open his church during COVID, and his full-time worship leader disagreed. She decided to move back to her home state until the virus died down. She posted lengthy Facebook comments on several occasions bashing him for keeping the church open. She claimed it was a mistake and accused him of not caring about people's lives. She drove many people out of the church. The pastor tried to keep the peace and kept her on staff, and then she left.

I know a pastor who had an evangelist in to preach, and his daughter missed the meeting. The pastor told the evangelist she missed the meetings due to a disease that made her tired, so the evangelist told him to bring her to the meeting so she would be healed. The pastor's adult daughter agreed to come, the evangelist prayed for her to be healed of the disease, and she was delivered. After the service, the pastor's daughter asked to speak with the evangelist, and she confessed that she never had a disease. She'd been fatigued from doing drugs with a member of the worship team.

The pastors in both stories are the same. The worship leader in the first story was doing drugs with the pastor's daughter. The common thread in both stories is the lack of confrontation.

If you let a cobra loose in your house, it doesn't just let itself out. You either cut the head off the snake, or it will start killing people in your home. Don't tolerate sin. If the Lord warns you about someone, confront them. My grandfather used to say, "Problems in life are free. You don't need to put them on the payroll." Often, the most significant problem people face in their business or ministry is the people they pay. Get rid of them, and figure out what to do after they're gone. Paying to keep a problem is the definition of stupidity.

Uncommon achievers confront sin. Don't be an Eli who allowed his sons to have sex with women in the temple and eat the offering before it was sacrificed to the Lord. When Eli's sons were confronted, they'd yell back, and Eli did nothing to remove them from their position. My dad once took me to the bathroom and paddled me while he was preaching. It was embarrassing, but he refused to let me misbehave in church.

That anonymous pastor I used as an example is certainly not unique. The Eli Syndrome is a common problem. How are you oblivious to the fact your daughter is on drugs? Remain sensitive to your family in your spirit. Don't have a word for every stranger while being disconnected when it comes to your family—that's the Eli Syndrome. If you get an intuition about something from the Lord, deal with it. Don't let anything go—confront it.

SECRET 37

UNCOMMON ACHIEVERS THINK ABOUT WAYS TO GENERATE MONEY, NOT WAYS TO SAVE MONEY

"Be careful to obey all the commands I am giving you today. Then you will live and multiply, and you will enter and occupy the land the Lord swore to give your ancestors. Remember how the Lord your God led you through the wilderness for these forty years, humbling you and testing you to prove your character, and to find out whether or not you would obey his commands. Yes, he humbled you by letting you go hungry and then feeding you with manna, a food previously unknown to you and your ancestors. He did it to teach you that people do not live by bread alone; rather, we live by every word that comes from the mouth of the Lord. For all these forty years your clothes didn't wear out, and your feet didn't blister or swell. Think about it: Just as a parent disciplines a child, the Lord your God disciplines you for your own good. So obey the commands of the Lord your God by walking in his ways and fearing him. For the Lord your God is bringing you into a good land of flowing streams and pools of water, with fountains and springs that gush out in the valleys and hills. It is a land of wheat and barley; of grapevines, fig trees, and pomegranates; of olive oil and honey. It is a land where food is plentiful and nothing is lacking. It is a land where iron is as common as stone, and copper is abundant in the hills. When you have eaten your fill, be sure to praise the Lord your God for the good land he has given you. But that is the time to be careful! Beware that in your plenty you do not forget the Lord your God and disobey his commands, regulations, and decrees that I am giving you today. For when you have become full and prosperous and have built fine homes to live in, and when your flocks and herds have become very large and your silver and gold have multiplied along with everything else, be careful! Do not become proud at that time and forget the Lord your God, who rescued you from slavery in the land of Egypt. Do not forget that he led you through the great and terrifying wilderness with its poisonous snakes and scorpions, where it was so hot and dry. He gave you water from the rock! He fed you with manna in the wilderness, a food unknown to your ancestors. He did this to humble you and test you for your own good. He did all this so you would never say to yourself, 'I have achieved this wealth with my own strength and energy.' Remember the Lord your God. He is the one who gives you power to be successful, in order to fulfill the covenant he confirmed to your ancestors with an oath."

— DEUTERONOMY 8:1-18

Uncommon achievers think of ways to generate revenue rather than how to save money. The King James translation of Deuteronomy 8:18 reads, *"Always remember it is the Lord your God who giveth thee power to create wealth."* Don't just think about how to save money. If coupon clippers used the time they spent clipping brainstorming ways to generate income, many would be multimillionaires. Quit wasting your God-given brain thinking of ways to save eighty bucks and use it to strategize ways to generate millions of dollars.

I know of ministers who oversaw the construction of their church to save money on hiring a general contractor. They took it upon themselves to ensure they didn't get taken advantage of by vendors. Once the building was completed, they took eighteen months off from preaching to manage the project. They ended up completely burned out because they spent three years framing, wiring, plumbing, and hanging drywall when God never called them to do it. In their effort to save money, they lost sight of their God-given assignments.

It's true that no one will watch over a project as thoroughly as the person paying, but the trade-off is having a dried-up ministry.

Saving money is not an accomplishment. I've read many biographies of uncommon achievers, and not one of them mentions anyone's superior ability to save money. They all highlight what was built and produced by great people. God never said, "I give you power to save money;" He said, "I give you power to create money." It's a shame to use your anointed mind to think of ways to save money instead of generating money. It's a mentality. Allow the Lord to take the power He gave you to create wealth and use it.

SECRET 38

UNCOMMON ACHIEVERS DO THINGS THAT HAVE NEVER BEEN DONE BEFORE

Uncommon achievers do things that have never been done before, or they do something in a way that has never been done. When you're the first to do something, it will take off. There's nothing wrong with drawing inspiration from different sources. Matthew Ashimolowo, senior pastor of Kingsway International Christian Centre in London, says that a pastor is like a bee that gathers pollen from different flowers and uses it to build its own hive. You'll find good ideas from other places—it's unavoidable. If you want to be uncommon, you have to either do something that's never been done before or do something in a way that's never been done before.

The story of Solomon building the temple for God is an example of this principle. No one had ever built a temple of such magnitude for any god. It was a building that's still worthy of mentioning to this day. I don't know exactly how much it would be worth today, but it included 112 tons of gold and 262 tons of silver. That amount of precious materials is worth tens of billions of dollars today. Solomon did something that had never been done before.

Check the News is not the first news program ever created. What makes it unique is the way we present news. Conservative news is typically depressing and humorless. News pundits always report news in a way that makes viewers feel like the world is ending, the dollar is crashing, and the Earth is out of oil. Watching conservative news makes you feel like you're about to die.

During the COVID lockdowns, when *Check the News* first began, circumstances were dire. Every program claimed America was failing, vaccine lockdowns were inevitable, and Walmart stores would be turned into concentration camps. That might have been the plan, but it didn't happen. *Check the News* reported the same news, but we made fun of everybody. The news was dire, but we reported it in a way that made people laugh. When you do something new or different, everyone will start copying it.

The Daily Show, hosted by John Stewart, was the first comedy news show. Now, all late-night talk shows have become news comedy shows, and most are awful, but the original was great.

If you sell a product that's not particularly unique, God can give you an idea to do it in a way that's completely different from all your competition, putting you ahead of the pack. Abraham was a cattle rancher who did something no one had ever done. He wasn't the only person who raised cattle, but he did something different from all the other people who were ranching cattle. He dug wells. Back then, everyone journeyed to find water for their livestock. God revealed to Abraham that there was water under the earth, and he used the water to irrigate his land. In drought, at times when everyone else's land was in famine, he was unaffected.

SECRET 39

UNCOMMON ACHIEVERS VALUE TIME

And it came to pass in the four hundred and eightieth year after the children of Israel were come out of the land of Egypt, in the fourth year of Solomon's reign over Israel, in the month Zif, which is the second month, that he began to build the house of the Lord.

— 1 KINGS 6:1 (KJV)

And I sent messengers unto them, saying, I am doing a great work, so that I cannot come down: why should the work cease, whilst I leave it, and come down to you?

— NEHEMIAH 6:3 (KJV)

If you want to become an uncommon achiever, you need to value time. Appointments need a start and end time. Never put yourself in a position where you can't control the time.

Restaurants are good places to meet people, but you must manage your time. People meet at restaurants for special events and to socialize, and they often linger. Most restaurant patrons would be upset if their meals came quickly and were rushed. When you attend an anniversary or retirement party, the staff assumes you want to be there for a long time.

I know a minister who calls restaurants ahead, orders his food, and tells them to put it on the table when he arrives. When I first heard that, I thought it was crazy, but the older I get, the more value I see in that practice. If you're wise, you value time and don't meet people in their homes.

If I invest money in something that I think will make a profit, but it tanks instead, I still own those shares. I can get money back over time or withdraw it and invest it in something else and double it. I cannot get time back. People who don't achieve anything in life place little value on their time. They're happy to talk to you all day. The more you achieve, the more valuable your time becomes. When I was younger, I was not aware of this secret. No one was happier to blow time doing nothing than me. People who knew you when you had all the time in the world will get upset now that you don't. If people can't understand your priorities, they need to be part of a ministry that has all the time in the world.

If you meet President Donald Trump, you better get to the point in about ninety seconds. Oral Roberts told the story of when he met President John F. Kennedy Jr. They were supposed to have thirty minutes together, but his brother, Robert Kennedy, interrupted the meeting with a serious look on his face and some papers and said, "This demands your attention right now." So, he had to cut the meeting short.

I remember my grandfather used to walk straight back to his office without breaking stride when he finished preaching. You could talk to him if you wanted, but you needed to walk out with him. I'm like that now. Most times, I have to catch a flight right after I finish preaching. I would love to stay and talk to everyone, but I don't have time. I'm on a mission.

The Bible says, *"Despise not the day of small beginnings"* (Zechariah 4:10). It also says, *"Your latter end will greatly increase"* (Job 8:7). Enjoy the phase of life that grants you an abundance of time. Don't allow yourself to become frustrated.

When my cousin first started in ministry, he was frustrated that he didn't have a meeting to preach for three weeks. I gave him the same advice. I told him to enjoy it, play video games, and relax because the time will come when those days will end, and he won't have time to do those things.

The day will come when you have a lot to do. Enjoy the present when you have weekends free. Enjoy your current stage and keep working toward growth. Someday, you'll need to say no to appointments. You'll have to learn to respond like Nehemiah when he said, *"I am engaged in a great work, so I can't come. Why should I stop working to come and meet with you?"*

(Nehemiah 6:3). Solomon valued time. Nehemiah valued time. All uncommon achievers value time.

You rarely see Dr. Rodney Howard-Browne outside of two places: his house and his church—that's it. You don't see him at restaurants. He built a restaurant in his church, complete with a chef and a full commercial kitchen.

Poor people have all the time in the world. If you ever get around uncommon achievers, their time is scheduled, and they handle it carefully. Most of the time, you won't even realize they have another meeting; they'll do something tricky to get you out of their office.

SECRET 40

UNCOMMON ACHIEVERS HIRE THE BEST OF THE BEST

King Solomon then asked for a man named Huram to come from Tyre. He was half Israelite, since his mother was a widow from the tribe of Naphtali, and his father had been a craftsman in bronze from Tyre. Huram was extremely skillful and talented in any work in bronze, and he came to do all the metal work for King Solomon.

— 1 KINGS 7:13-14

Uncommon achievers hire the best of the best. You have two choices when hiring people: you can hire someone who will give you a deal or hire high-quality people and pay them high-quality wages. You need to pay well to keep good people, or they'll leave because everyone wants and deserves to increase. Solomon hired the best of the best.

Not everyone has an established reputation when you hire them. The Holy Spirit will give you discernment. I didn't hire the best office administrator in the country. I didn't hire Joyce Meyer or John Hagee's office administrator. I hired Magalis because I could see a gift in her. When someone has a gift, they can be trained, and they will figure things out. Now, I would put Magalis up against anybody. The same is true for Patrick, who handles our finances.

I wasn't the best preacher when I was thirty-one, but I had a gift. My staff and I have learned and grown together. At the same time, it's not the worst idea to find the best people for the positions you need. In the corporate world, they call it headhunting. Find out who's the best. Many Christians feel like they're limited to hiring based on local availability. My father approached a broadcasting school, requested their top student, and hired him out of college. You're not limited by where you live. You can hire the best of the best regardless of geographic location. Huram wasn't even of the Jewish faith. He was from Tyre and was half Israelite, half pagan. Solomon didn't hire him for his beliefs; he hired him because he was well-skilled in bronze work.

I don't care how much our airplane pilots pray. I prefer never to hear them pray. It would make me nervous to hear tongues coming from the cockpit. I'd assume the plane was violently on its way to the ground. My only concern is how effective my pilot is at landing and taking off.

I'm not interested in a surgeon's devotional life. If someone I know needs surgery, I want the best surgeon. Why is it that

Christians always want to tell you about how good someone's heart is, as if it's an excuse for how terrible they are at their job. If you have a great heart, run a marathon or tell your cardiologist. A good heart is not a requirement for a sound engineer.

The guy who handled sound for our outdoor crusades wasn't a Christian. He ended up getting saved after the fourth crusade we hosted after he witnessed a lady healed of cerebral palsy. He cried and received salvation. Before working with our ministry, he was a rock and roll soundman. He ran sound for Billy Joel, and he did excellent work. Our current soundman is a Christian, but I didn't hire Devin for that reason. If he backslid, I still would have hired him because I want a good soundman.

On the other hand, if you're in the ministry, you don't just hire a good musician to lead praise and worship. Certain positions require someone who's saved, but if you're in business, hire people who are excellent at their work.

One way the Devil shipwrecks people's dreams and keeps their achievements small is by preying on the merciful and compassionate nature of Christians. You didn't start a business to double as a rehab clinic. When we took mission trips to Hawaii to plant churches, I told the locals we were not running a rehab clinic. Our church was not a place to send troubled teens. I wanted top-notch Christian youth and young adults to assist me in building the church and winning people to the Lord. You need to make a choice. Do you want a construction company that's equal parts methadone clinic, rehab, and general contractor, or do you want a construction company that's a multimillion-dollar success?

Hire excellent people. Hire the best of the best. Solomon didn't hire his nephew to do bronze work; he hired someone from Tyre, whose father was not an Israelite but had a reputation for excellent bronze work. You have internet access. Go online and figure out who's the best.

SECRET 41

UNCOMMON ACHIEVERS DON'T TOLERATE DISLOYALTY

Uncommon achievers don't tolerate disloyalty. In 2 Samuel, chapters 13 to 19, we read of the initial signs of dissent in David's rule. David's son, Absalom, rebelled and sought to overthrow his father and take the throne for himself. He gathered support from the people and began a rebellion against David's reign. When David learned of Absalom's intentions, he fled Jerusalem. David's timid response to Absalom's disloyalty marked a significant decline in his rule. Just as Eli tolerated disloyalty from his sons, it came at a great cost to David as well.

In 1 Kings 2:14-25, we see a great contrast in how Solomon dealt with disloyalty when his brother, Adonijah, rebelled against his authority. In verse 25, Solomon ordered his death. Solomon dealt harshly with Adonijah's disloyalty even though he was his brother. Solomon refused to tolerate the slightest disloyalty. If you catch somebody being disloyal and you don't deal with it, you will have a problem.

 You can't turn a wolf into a sheep.

Jesus taught about sheep, wolves, and wolves in sheep's clothing (Matthew 7:15). The longer you're in ministry, the quicker you'll be able to spot wolves dressed as sheep. Those kinds of people have similar spirits. A lady willing to commit adultery with someone on staff at a church has the same spirit—she's a wolf dressed like a sheep. Your church could be based in Tacoma, Washington, or Dallas, Texas—the lady will have a different face but the same behavior and mannerisms. You can always spot a concealed wolf if you can discern spirits.

When my Uncle Tim was the associate pastor for my grandfather, a new family came to church one Sunday morning. My grandfather was getting ready to retire, and he pointed at the husband subtly and told my uncle to keep an eye on that family once he took over. He knew they were going to be trouble. My Uncle Tim thought my grandfather was passing harsh judgment, it being their first Sunday at church. But later, my uncle admitted the family had caused him all kinds of problems. When you reach your sixties, you can spot people.

Many Christians waste their whole life trying to turn a wolf into a sheep. After three and a half years of listening to Jesus teach and witnessing His miracles, even Jesus couldn't change Judas. So don't feel bad if you can't change a wolf. Jesus said, *"But one of you is a devil"* (John 6:70). However, if you think everyone around you is a devil, you're the one with the problem.

A friend of mine was invited to preach at a church, and the soundman yelled at the pastor's wife right in front of him. My friend expected the pastor to hit him for disrespecting his wife, but the pastor just stood there as the pastor's wife shook her head. Then the pastor excused the soundman's behavior by saying, "He loses his temper sometimes, but I don't know what we'd do if he left the church. He's one of our biggest givers." Satan will plant people in a church to keep it small, and pastors often bend over backward or forward to keep a wolf. In the meantime, you're allowing a wolf to run people off left and right. Not to mention, it's spiritually out of order.

One time, while Evangelist R.W. Schambach was laying hands on people and anointing them with oil, a lady started yelling at him before he could lay hands on her. "You spent over an hour on the offering tonight. These people have come to be healed." He was nice. He skipped her and kept praying. When he got three people down the line, the Lord told him, "If you don't deal with her, there won't be any more healings or miracles because she undercut your authority in the spirit." So, he went back and gave her a verbal thrashing. Then, he went back to praying for people.

I've learned many lessons about authority from my dad. He teaches that your authority is connected to your anointing. Allowing people to override your authority will inhibit your anointing because they've spiritually dethroned you.

Jesus never asked anyone to write a letter to the board of the church in Philadelphia. He gave instructions to write it to the angel of the church in Philadelphia. The angel is the leader.

There's a very famous ministry in the United States with a huge church. One brother was in line to have the church turned over to him when his father died, but at the last moment, while on his deathbed, he decided to give it to the younger son instead. The older brother acted the same way Absalom did. He tried to split the church by publishing dissenting blog posts. His behavior caused his whole ministry and life to fall apart. He ended up divorced and lost the church he started that met in a school on Saturdays because he could no longer afford the lease.

The Bible is full of patterns. When you identify which pattern someone follows, it enables you to understand their current behavior and predict their future behavior.

Mistakes are not disloyalty. If Rom, our media director, forgets to play a video, it's a mistake. You can tolerate mistakes but never tolerate disloyalty. Don't confuse the two and start firing people left and right. An example of disloyalty would be if Rom skipped prayer to host a separate prayer meeting in his home.

I mentioned shepherds, sheep, wolves, and wolves in sheep's clothing because Jesus mentioned them when teaching pastoral ministry. You need to know who's who—sheep are not shepherds. Pastors don't make group decisions.

A member of my uncle's church sounded off on my uncle with a list of complaints. When the guy finished his rant, my uncle looked up from behind his desk with a huge grin and said, "Here's what you don't understand. I'm a shepherd, and you're a sheep. You keep talking, but all I hear is 'Baaaaaaaaa.'" The man's face changed colors, and he left. People destroy their churches by allowing sheep to tend the work of shepherds. A good businessman doesn't make a good preacher, in the same way, an anointed pastor wouldn't necessarily run a successful construction or accounting business.

If you spot a wolf and get rid of them, you'll lose one person or family, but if you allow them to stay, they'll gather a following. When you're finally forced to address the issue, you'll lose many people. People often fail to understand that confrontation is inevitable. It's not a matter of *if* you'll face confrontation, only a matter of *when*. You can decide to remove someone the first day they begin causing problems, or you can wait until they assemble forty people and have begun their own Bible study or side business. You can wait even longer until they've gathered three-quarters of the congregation or workforce and vote you out of your own ministry or business. It's not an exaggeration—it's happened many times. Don't become another cautionary tale.

Uncommon achievers refuse to tolerate the slightest disloyalty. Deal with the problem, or the problem will deal with you. Cut the head off the snake when it's small. If you wait until it's big, it'll choke you out.

I was told a story about a husband and wife who were missionaries overseas. A small snake came into their house, and they treated it like a pet, even allowing it to get into bed with them at night. Eventually, they shared the story of their pet snake with a local. They fondly described how the snake was growing bigger and bigger in their care. The local insisted that they kill the snake immediately because it was growing bigger in preparation to eat them after it choked them to death in their sleep. That's how people behave. They ignore small problems until they become big enough to ruin their lives.

I was invited to preach for a friend, and I ministered on obeying the voice of the Holy Spirit and the importance of immediately responding to God's instructions. Afterward, my friend told me the Lord reminded him of a check in his spirit against hiring their youth pastor, but he went through with it anyway because he didn't know who else to hire. Then the youth pastor's wife started throwing Tupperware parties in the church sanctuary, and when the pastor's wife told her she couldn't host private events in the church sanctuary, she posted her grievance on Facebook in all caps. She mentioned the pastor and his wife by name and accused them of being selfish. He kept them because he didn't want to deal with firing them. That night, what I preached reminded him that his youth pastor and his wife were out of the will of God, and he was out of the will of God for hiring them. Then he asked me what he should do. I told him to fire them both before nine o'clock tomorrow morning. Making a mistake is one thing, but maintaining the error is another level of stupidity. He listened and fired him the following day.

God speaks to the leader, and it's the leader's job to disseminate information to his team. God spoke to Moses—it was his responsibility to get everyone on board. When you're in charge, God holds you responsible. That's why ministers receive double honor, dual accountability, and double responsibility. God holds pastors accountable for what happens in the church.

This is a tricky concept to grasp if you were educated at New York University and majored in gender studies, but God is not a professor at New York University. His approach to and relationship with the Church reflects His order and structure of marriage. In the same way, the pastor is the head of the church, a husband is the high priest of the home, and a wife should submit to her husband as the Church submits to Christ.

SECRET 42

UNCOMMON ACHIEVERS HONOR THE LAW OF ADMIRATION

Achievers honor the law of admiration. Make sure you're not always the one talking. Listen to people who have accomplished more than you without telling them about your accomplishments—this is the law of admiration.

When I first met Jesse Duplantis, I was in the room with other preachers as Jesse told us a story about acquiring a plane. One preacher chimed in about how he acquired a new car. If he was smart, he would have shut up and listened. Preachers are some of the worst people on Earth when it comes to honoring the law of admiration—they always have to talk.

Some people have a list of ten preachers they don't like at the ready but can't name even one preacher they do like! If you don't admire anyone, you can't follow the scripture that instructs us to be *"followers of them who through faith and patience inherit the promises"* (Hebrews 6:12). The Bible doesn't just tell you to follow God; it commands you to follow or imitate those who have obtained God's promises. The only way to obey this instruction is to identify people who have obtained the promises of God. Always know who the top person is in every room. If it's not you, keep your mouth shut. Honor the law of admiration.

Lester Sumrall chaired Billy Graham's crusade in South Bend, Indiana. When Billy Graham came to meet him, Dr. Sumrall prepared to introduce himself, and Billy Graham said, "Dr. Lester Sumrall, I've been looking forward to meeting you." Billy Graham was a Baptist. It wasn't unfair to assume he wouldn't have known about Full Gospel preachers.

Surprised, Dr. Sumrall asked, "You know me?" Billy Graham replied, "Oh yeah, I've been following you for a long time. I watch you on television. I've made it my business to find the people in my generation whom God is using and pray for them."

That's Billy Graham. There's a term in the Bible that many are familiar with, but most don't understand what it means: *meekness*. Meekness is the ability to be teachable. If you lack meekness, you don't read any books. You don't speak with people on the phone to learn about what they know. You're always the one talking.

Moses met with God the Father on a mountain, yet when his father-in-law sat him down and provided him wise advice about governing, he took note and implemented it. He didn't combat the advice just because he spoke with God on a mountain. The Bible says Moses was the meekest man in all the Earth.

> Now the man Moses was very meek, above all the men which were upon the face of the earth.
>
> — NUMBERS 12:3 (KJV)

Honor the law of admiration. Great people meet with other great people. It's one of the secrets of their success. Whatever you do for work, whatever your dream is, make it your business to know who is the best in the field. Once you identify who it is, meet with them. People at the top usually have forums to teach what they know. Why haven't you met them? You can learn more in one conversation than forty years of formal learning if you speak to the right person. You don't have to attend the school of hard knocks, but if you choose not to read any books or meet with people smarter than you, that's your only option.

Most preachers won't sit in another preacher's service. The only time they go to church is if they're preaching. They have no interest in hearing what anyone else has to say, and that's why they stay small.

Earlier, I mentioned the importance of hiring the best. I've modeled that in who I invite to preach at Revival Today Church. I only invite five-star ministers in to preach. I'm not asking my buddy to share some thoughts just to fill my pulpit while I visit my parents in Maine. I seek out the best of the best.

Your business is not a charity. Though your ministry has charitable status, it is not a charity either—it's a serious endeavor, and you should treat it as such. Be serious about who you hire. Be serious about your time. Take your life seriously because you only get one—you're not a Grand Theft Auto character. You can't bank lives, hit the 'A' button, drop back down from the sky, and continue on. Do the things that are in your heart to do and do them with excellence.

 Take your life, calling, and assignment very seriously.

Seeing an angel when I was eight years old has helped me. It's a constant reminder that one day, I'll enter the heavenly realm and give an account of what I've done in this body. I'm not interested in how people feel about how I use my time or what they think of my course of action. I'm interested in hearing, *"Well done, my good and faithful servant."*

When you stand before the Lord, either He'll show you what He had planned for your life, and it will be ninety times greater than what you accomplished, or He'll show you what he had planned, but because you excelled and did well with what He gave you, He continued to add more. You can end up doing more than He originally intended. He'll add the assignments of unfaithful servants to your destiny. Which one do you want to hear?

I'm going to accomplish my mission. People's feelings are irrelevant to me, and they change constantly. The person criticizing you today will return ten years later to tell you they're sorry. People will lay palm branches down before you and a few days later say, "Give us Barabbas and kill Jesus." People are fickle, which is why their feelings shouldn't concern you.

SECRET 43

UNCOMMON ACHIEVERS DO NOT ASSUME THE BEST OF EVERYONE IN THE AREA OF FINANCES

"Look, I am sending you out as sheep among wolves.
So be as shrewd as snakes and harmless as doves."

— MATTHEW 10:16

Uncommon achievers don't assume the best of everyone in the area of finances. Jesus instructed us to *"be as wise as serpents, but as harmless as doves"* (Matthew 10:16). Most Christians get an A+ in the harmless as doves part and an F- when it comes to being as wise as serpents. Most churches teach people to assume the best of everyone.

At around twelve years old, my mother-in-law had a feeling that the Catholic priest in her parish molested children. When she told her parents, they gave her a sound beating and sent her away to live with someone else. They were angry because it wasn't permitted to speak negatively about a priest. I'm not suggesting people should disrespect those in authority, but in this case, my mother-in-law was right.

The Devil uses niceties against many Christians. It's always been foolish to assume the best of anyone, but it's particularly foolish in this day and age. If something hits you wrong, pay attention to it.

While sitting with His disciples, Jesus said, *"But one of you is a devil."* You don't have to assume the worst in people, but don't assume the best in everyone either, and never override your spiritual intuition. It's a mistake the Devil will use against you. I know people who have had their families destroyed because they were so loving that they took homeless drifters from the church into their homes. The next thing you know, one of them molested their child. It's a mistake to assume the best in everyone.

Uncommon achievers do not assume the best in everyone in the realm of finances. You are breaking this law by letting the same two people count the offering every Sunday. It wouldn't take much for two people to conspire to steal from the offering, and if they do, you're in big trouble. You should have at least six people rotate to count your church's offerings. It's even better to have nine or twelve people, but never have less than three people counting. It's also a wise idea to have cameras in the room where the money is counted.

 Very few people can be around money and not steal it.

We use our own offering envelopes in our meetings now, but we didn't when we first started out. Amazingly, once we started using our own, our offerings tripled. Maybe there's a special anointing on our envelopes, but it's more likely that people stole the large checks from the offering when we didn't use our own envelopes.

After we started using our own envelopes, one church handed them to my nephew already opened with cash and checks in them. When my nephew showed it to me, I called the pastor and asked him why the envelopes were returned to us opened. I don't even open them. A team of people count them in a room with cameras. He claimed he needed a count to report to his denomination for mission giving. That's not acceptable. I told him if it ever happened again, I would leave and never return. It doesn't matter if he trusts the people who count the offering—I don't know them, therefore I don't trust them. They may be very nice people, but counting money in a back room with the door locked with no cameras is not wise. No one with an IQ north of room temperature should trust that setup.

You don't put someone who might be two mortgage payments behind in a room with $14,000 cash. You don't know what people are going through. That's quite a temptation to place before someone. Your carelessness can put people in a tempting situation.

Uncommon achievers take drastic safeguards in the realm of finance. Very few people can be around money and not steal it. Jesus' treasurer routinely stole from the treasury.

There's only so much you can do. It's possible for someone to steal money from my ministry, but they would need to get my wife, Patrick, and my wife's twin sister, Magalis, all in on it. At that point, my ministry would be over anyway if my own wife conspired with thieves to steal from my ministry. There are only so many safeguards you can take, but you better have enough of them in place to thwart temptation. In the realm of money, you should assume the worst in everyone. Very few people can be around money and not steal it. This doesn't just apply to ministries. If you run a business, you better have serious safeguards regarding your cash register and your deposit protocols.

A friend of mine heard me teach this, and afterward, he told me he suspected the woman he put in charge of counting and depositing the church offerings of stealing. I told him he had a bad system in place. I suggested that he present her with an opportunity to tend to more important church matters, almost like a promotion. As a result, it takes the responsibility of counting and depositing church money away and gives it to someone else to free her up for the increase in her responsibilities. If she gets angry for being given less work for the same pay, he'd know she was stealing.

Sure enough, when he very kindly told her he would remove the responsibility, she flipped out. He wasn't taking away responsibility; he was taking away a source of income from a thief. This is a prime example of why uncommon achievers take drastic safeguards in the realm of finances and cash.

SECRET 44

UNCOMMON ACHIEVERS DON'T ASSUME THE BEST OF PEOPLE OR THEIR MOTIVES

> Behold, I send you forth as sheep in the midst of wolves: be ye therefore wise as serpents, and harmless as doves.
>
> — MATTHEW 10:16 (KJV)

Uncommon achievers don't assume the best of people or their motives, and there are three character flaws that they do not tolerate.

3 CHARACTER FLAWS TO AVOID AT ALL COSTS

Liars

If you ever catch someone in a lie, get rid of them immediately. Don't even bother to confront them.

Never confront a liar.

Confronting a liar is equivalent to backing a cobra into a corner. Don't do it—just get rid of them. You don't have to tell someone the reason you're firing them. Satan is not called the Father of Adultery. Satan is not called the Father of Homosexuality. Satan is not called the Father of Theft. Satan is the Father of Lies. Jesus is The Truth. Lying is not a small offense —it's a satanic quality. If you catch someone in a lie, don't wait for them to tell you another. Treat a liar like a cobra. Liars are dangerous people; remove them immediately.

Unthankful People

Get rid of unthankful people. They have a problem, and they will become your problem in the future. Unthankfulness is rooted in entitlement, and entitlement is the breeding ground for theft. An unthankful person feels entitled to more. Maybe you pay them $41,000 a year, but they think they should be making at least $60,000, and because they're not thankful for the $41,000, they subconsciously feel justified in stealing $19,000 worth of your stuff. Thieves never feel they've done anything wrong. Do you think people who steal feel convicted while they shoplift? They feel no guilt or remorse because they believe they're entitled to it. They think that because of their race, upbringing, or the way they've been treated, they have a right to steal. An unthankful person is an entitled person, and entitlement will breed theft. If they haven't already stolen, they will steal at some point.

Unhappy People

The Bible says, *"Happy are the people whose God is the Lord"* (Psalm 144:15). Of all the people I've known who have fallen into sin, whether they were ministers or businesspeople, they've all had one thing in common: they were not happy. Sin makes people unhappy.

Jesse Duplantis said, "When you're not a Christian, money will make you comfortable while you're miserable." Look out for miserable people. If I had an unhappy receptionist, I'd get rid of her. I don't care why people are unhappy—there's always a reason, but there's a problem if you're not happy.

I talked to a pastor recently whose wife passed away a few hours after I spoke to him. She was with a hospice nurse when I called. He had a joyful conversation with me. We laughed on the phone while he was in the room with his wife of around sixty years. Christians are happy people. Christians have joy. I know that's somehow a novel concept. Paul was beaten with rods and thrown in prison, and he prayed and sang praises. He wasn't singing somber, sad worship songs—he sang upbeat, happy, joyous praise to the Lord.

If you want to separate yourself from the crowd, tell the truth, be grateful, and be happy. You'll have no shortage of open doors.

SECRET 45

UNCOMMON ACHIEVERS KNOW WHAT THEY'RE CALLED TO DO AND RECOGNIZE WHAT THEY'RE NOT CALLED TO DO

> For I speak to you Gentiles; inasmuch as I am an apostle to the Gentiles, I magnify my ministry, if by any means I may provoke to jealousy those who are my flesh and save some of them.
>
> — ROMANS 11:13-14 (NKJV)

Uncommon achievers know what they're called to do and recognize what they're not called to do. Anytime Paul attempted to reach the Jewish people, it was an abysmal failure. Sure, when Paul tried to reach Gentiles, he was thrown in prison, but God broke him out. When he tried to reach the Jewish people, he was arrested and had to hire a lawyer or appeal to a higher legal authority through earthly means—there was no grace on his effort.

Uncommon achievers know what they're not called to do. Paul figured out he wasn't just an apostle—he was an apostle sent to the Gentiles. He loved the Jewish people, but they were not his assignment.

Uncommon achievers recognize what they're not called to do. Chick-fil-A doesn't make pizza. I'd like to know how many people have tried to convince Chick-fil-A to make burgers. McDonald's lost money trying to make too many things. At one point, they had seventy-two items on their menu. Do you think someone making nine dollars an hour knows how to cook seventy-two menu items?

 Just because there's a need doesn't mean it's your assignment.

If you're in business or ministry, there are always a zillion things that need attention, and they're all seemingly important, but they're not necessarily what you're called to do. Human trafficking victims need rescuing, but if it's not what you're called to do, you'll waste a lot of time and money and have a tough time.

Bishop David Oyedepo said, "If your church is not called to build a hospital, and you build one anyway, you may be the first patient." Anytime you do what you're not called to do, you do it outside God's grace, and it will wear you down. Just because there's a need doesn't mean it's your assignment.

People need Bibles in the Arctic. Human trafficked victims need to be rescued. Japan has very few churches. We could list a hundred things that are pertinent to the Gospel, but you need to know your assignment and recognize what's not your assignment.

SECRET 46

UNCOMMON ACHIEVERS ARE GENEROUS PEOPLE

The liberal soul shall be made fat: and he that watereth shall be watered also himself.

— PROVERBS 11:25 (KJV)

Uncommon achievers are generous people. Generosity puts you into a financial flow you would otherwise have to work hard to achieve. We sent a $65,000 tithe from our ministry to Jesse Duplantis. Within forty-eight hours, we received a check for $225,000, one for $5,000, and another for $50,000. That's just under $300,000 in total. Seed produces a harvest. *"For with the same measure that you use, it will be measured back to you"* (Luke 6:38). The person who gave the $225,000 didn't know we had just given $65,000; they had never even given to our ministry before.

Two weeks later, our tithe was around $80,000. I added a $20,000 seed to round it up to $100,000. The day after I went to see Brother Jesse Duplantis with that check for $100,000, we received a check in the mail from a lady who had never given before. She wrote, "I'm sending my tithe of $50,000 and a second check as an offering of $100,000." Who gives an offering that's double their tithe? That lady does!

We gave $100,000 and received $150,000 less than twelve hours after we sowed it. When the Lord put it on my heart to sow $100,000, unknown to me, $150,000 was already waiting for me in the mailbox. When God speaks to you to give, it tests what you're willing to walk away from. Anything you're willing to walk away from, God will give back to you a hundredfold, according to Mark 10:30. Solomon, David, and Abraham were all generous men. Jesus gave and gave and gave until He gave His own blood. Your seed produces your harvest. The reason so much money flows into our ministry is because we're a sowing ministry. At the time of this writing, we've given over $6 million this year to other ministries and ministers, and we've been gifted a plane, building, and acreage.

What you give always comes back to you. *"The liberal soul shall be made fat: and he that watereth shall be watered also himself"* (Proverbs 11:25). Your gift doesn't come back to you the same; it comes back one hundredfold. It keeps coming and coming and coming. If you sow $6 million, you don't get $6 million in return; it comes back multiplied.

You rarely reap where you sow. When I gave *to* Jesse Duplantis, I received no money *from* Jesse Duplantis. I gave *to* Rodney

Howard-Browne, but the money didn't come back *from* him. Jesus instructed us not to give like the heathen do. They give to those whom they know can pay them back. You're not giving to open doors—that's bribery.

When I invited Brother Jesse to preach at our church, I made sure he knew my seed wasn't a bribe. He's welcome to never preach here again, and I'd still sow again. Dr. Rodney is welcome to never do another thing for me, and I'd sow again.

You rarely reap where you've sown. *"He who gives to the poor lends to the Lord, and the Lord will repay him for his deed"* (Proverbs 19:17). Ephesians 6:8 says, *"Whatsoever good any man doeth the same shall he also receive of the Lord, whether he be bond or free."*

Many people don't sow, and of those who do, many don't understand the supernatural aspect. Because their heart isn't right, they don't receive any reward for their giving. I'm an evangelist. Very few evangelists give to someone if they aren't invited back to preach within two years of giving a large offering. They attempt to reap where they sow, which is unscriptural. When you make good things happen for others, the Lord will make better things happen for you. The people who gifted us our building testified to the phenomenal growth they've experienced in their business. They said, "We could only trace it back to giving this building."

I sent a pastor's wife five thousand dollars after her husband was put in jail for keeping his church open during COVID. I would want someone to ensure my wife was taken care of if that happened to me. Not long after, someone set up an account for my daughter to receive five hundred thousand dollars when she turns eighteen. I'm not the best at math, but that sounds like a hundred-fold return to me. It's an unbreakable law. What you make happen for others, God makes happen for you.

Many people lack because they've never given a substantial offering. I gave my first $1,000 at twenty-one years old when I only had $1,100 to my name. Don't wait until you have $10 million in the bank to sow $1,000.

SECRET 47

UNCOMMON ACHIEVERS CAN WORK WITH THOSE THEY DON'T FULLY AGREE WITH

"I am sending you a master craftsman named Huramabi, who is extremely talented. His mother is from the tribe of Dan in Israel, and his father is from Tyre. He is skillful at making things from gold, silver, bronze, and iron, and he also works with stone and wood. He can work with purple, blue, and scarlet cloth and fine linen. He is also an engraver and can follow any design given to him. He will work with your craftsmen and those appointed by my lord David, your father. Send along the wheat, barley, olive oil, and wine that my lord has mentioned."

— 2 CHRONICLES 2:13-15

Uncommon achievers can work with those they don't fully agree with. Solomon chose the most skilled people to build the Temple. They were not Israelites; they were Gentiles who didn't believe in the God of Israel, but that didn't matter. Losers look for differences; leaders look for commonality.

I listen to a man on YouTube who predicts how the Supreme Court will rule, and he's rarely ever wrong. He was anti-mask and anti-lockdown during the so-called pandemic. He's also an atheist who uses 666 in his YouTube name. Most preachers wouldn't listen to his advice once they discover he's an atheist, especially once they see he has 666 in his username, but those things don't bother me because I don't listen to him for spiritual advice. I listened to his predictions on whether the OSHA vaccine mandate would be upheld or struck down, and he nailed it. He predicted it would be struck down by a vote of 6:3, and that's exactly what happened.

I can work with a Buddhist if they're against government infringement on free speech and religious freedom easier than I can tolerate a Christian minister who thinks the government should be allowed to shut down churches. I don't have to agree with someone on everything to work with them; I just need to agree on our task.

When I board a plane, I don't care who the pilots voted for in the last election; I care if they can fly the aircraft. I'm not concerned with the state of their prayer life or where they go to church. I don't care if they're baptized in the Holy Ghost or if they believe in a pre-tribulation rapture. I care that they can get the plane airborne and land it at my desired destination.

Many Christians live in a tiny world because they'll only deal with anti-mask, anti-vaccine, Holy Ghost-filled, pre-tribulation rapture people. You won't talk to too many people if you operate like this. Learn to find common ground with people without selling out your values. If you're going to impact the world, you must work with the world.

If you're going to disengage from every brand and business that supports things that don't align with your beliefs, you'll die. You'd have to leave Earth or start a commune where you manufacture all your own products. If you trace anything back far enough, you'll find a reason not to patronize them. Uncommon achievers can work with people they don't see eye to eye with one hundred percent.

SECRET 48

UNCOMMON ACHIEVERS ARE NOT ENTITLED PEOPLE

Uncommon achievers are not entitled people. The world owes me nothing, and it doesn't owe you anything either. When you're not entitled, you'll always be surprised when someone does something nice for you because you're not expecting anything. You're focused on how you can help others.

My parents have a nice home. When they sell it or pass away, they're free to take the money, put it in a dumpster, and burn it. They're free to donate it to the World Wildlife Federation or do whatever they want because they don't owe me anything.

Losers always talk about what someone didn't do for them. No one has to do anything for you. You're responsible for your life the same way I am responsible for my life. I will give an account to the Lord for my life, and there won't be anyone to blame.

Imagine if Joseph felt entitled and sat in prison and stewed over how his brothers treated him. His story would have turned out differently, but he chose to move forward.

> "For even the Son of Man came not to be served but to serve others and to give his life as a ransom for many."
>
> — MATTHEW 20:28

Follow Christ's example. Christ came to *pour His life out*. Uncommon achievers are celebrated for pouring their life out. No one celebrates people based on what they were given. People are celebrated for what they've given to others. If your goal is to collect from people, you'll never stand out in life.

SECRET 49

UNCOMMON ACHIEVERS UNDERSTAND THEY WILL LOSE WHAT THEY DON'T PROTECT

> Hezekiah received the Babylonian envoys and showed them everything in his treasure-houses—the silver, the gold, the spices, and the aromatic oils. He also took them to see his armory and showed them everything in his royal treasuries! There was nothing in his palace or kingdom that Hezekiah did not show them.
>
> — 2 KINGS 20:13

Uncommon achievers understand they will lose what they don't protect. If you have a passing knowledge of the Bible, you know Babylon was not friendly toward God's people. Hezekiah had the grand idea to show the Babylonian envoy his entire treasury. The Bible says there wasn't anything he didn't show them.

In Jeremiah 25, the Babylonians regrouped after the death of Hezekiah. Hezekiah was unique because the Lord told him what the Babylonians would do and that it wouldn't happen in his lifetime. The Bible says he wasn't worried about it because he knew he wouldn't be alive to deal with the consequences. He had no thought of subsequent generations.

 What you don't protect, you will lose.

If you invite your enemy into your home and show them where all your money is, you will get robbed. I don't even open my door to accept food from my DoorDash or Uber Eats driver. I have them leave it at the door. I don't need someone with a heroin problem coming to my entryway, handing me my food, and peeking at what's inside.

What you don't protect, you will lose. If you don't protect your marriage, you'll lose it. If you don't protect your children, you'll lose them. You will lose your business and your money if you don't protect it. I take my obligation to protect seriously.

The first thing we did when we acquired our church building was secure it. If someone breaks into our offices, I'm not interested in watching the assailant on video. I want the place locked down so intruders can't break in and steal.

Our church and congregation are protected. The first-ever church shooting was understandable. After twenty years of frequent church shootings, the blame belongs to the pastor. As a minister, it should be impossible for someone to enter your church and harm the congregation. Likewise, it should be impossible for a child to be molested or abducted from your children's ministry.

 The Devil attacks unprotected territory.

The Devil doesn't like to fight. He goes after soft targets. What you don't protect, you'll lose. If the Lord gives you a building, protect it. There was a church in the South that stayed open during the pandemic. The media made them a public target, and someone burned the church to the ground. Any church that defied the lockdown orders found itself at the center of nationwide scrutiny and reproach. The leadership of that church was under the influence of a spirit of poverty. How else can you explain the decision not to hire a security team to protect it?

God will not turn his sheep over to delinquent shepherds who don't protect their flock. Protect your business, your dream, your wife, and your children. You don't live in the millennium—lions are not lying down with lambs. You live in a dangerous world. What you don't protect, you *will* lose—there's no maybe about it. Our ministry takes every measure possible to protect what's entrusted to us.

SECRET 50

UNCOMMON ACHIEVERS NOTICE TRENDS— THEY DON'T WAIT FOR CRISES

When the Spirit of truth comes, he will guide you into all the truth, for he will not speak on his own authority, but whatever he hears he will speak, and he will declare to you the things that are to come.

— JOHN 16:13 (ESV)

Uncommon achievers notice trends; they don't wait for crisis. Sunday morning church attendance doesn't drop from 1,200 to 40 overnight. First, it decreases from 1,200 to 900, then from 900 to 800. As soon as you recognize the downtrend, make a correction. Too often, people wait until there's no money in the bank to say, "We've hit a crisis." Most people don't address a problem until it's become a crisis. Pay attention to trends and react promptly to them.

If our ministry experiences a decrease in giving for two consecutive weeks, I don't ignore it just because there's plenty of money in reserve. It may not have a negative impact at the moment, but I don't like the trend. I use that information to examine what we are doing. What have we been teaching? What are we doing differently? What is it that people are not responding to? Something needs to be fixed. Don't wait until you've hit rock bottom to address problems. Notice a bad week or month before it becomes a crisis.

It's also important to notice trends in people. Notice poor attitudes. Notice when your kids aren't raising their hands. You can apply the same principle to your finances and your children. Take notice of everything.

I wouldn't wait until Camila is living with an unsaved boyfriend to wonder what went wrong. I would notice well before the problem became so dire. If I were to ask everyone to stand up and lift their hands, she'd be the first one on her feet singing, but if one day she refused to get up, I would notice and address it after service. It's not hard to read people, but you need to be intentional in your observation and awareness. Notice changes in people.

Intentional observation goes hand in hand with protection. When you protect something, it's because you care about it. When you care about people, you pay attention to their behavior and demeanor. I spoke with a pastor who had several people leave his church. He told me that before leaving, they would gradually move from the front of the church to the back. Then, they stopped giving. Finally, they stopped coming. Notice changes in people and take action.

SECRET 51

UNCOMMON ACHIEVERS THINK GENERATIONALLY

> A good man leaveth an inheritance to his children's children: and the wealth of the sinner is laid up for the just.
>
> — PROVERBS 13:22 (KJV)

Uncommon achievers think generationally. What are you laying up for your grandchildren? After I'm gone, I want a Shuttlesworth road leading to a Shuttlesworth estate where Camila and her children live.

When the Lord told Hezekiah all the terrible things that would happen after his death, he couldn't have cared less. Common losers think only about the immediate. There is an adage that if you invest twenty dollars a week from the time you turn eighteen, you will retire a multimillionaire. So, why doesn't everyone do that? The answer is: because no one wants to wait forty-two years to spend their twenty dollars.

Uncommon achievers think generationally. Abraham left wealth to Isaac. He left generational wealth to his son and his grandson. David left riches to Solomon. He left Solomon a well-oiled machine and prepared him to step into his role as king. John Osteen did that for his son Joel.

Uncommon achievers think generationally. Common people can't see past this month or this week; they have no plan for the long term.

SECRET 52

UNCOMMON ACHIEVERS CAN GAIN THE WHOLE WORLD WITHOUT LOSING THEIR SOUL

> If you try to hang on to your life, you will lose it. But if you give up your life for my sake and for the sake of the Good News, you will save it. And what do you benefit if you gain the whole world but lose your own soul? Is anything worth more than your soul?
>
> — MARK 8:35-37

Uncommon achievers can gain the whole world without losing their soul. The higher God takes me, the harder I will press into Him.

We sang a song growing up in Pentecostal church: "Take the whole world but give me Jesus. I'd rather have Jesus than silver or gold. I'd rather have Him than riches untold." If I had to choose between riches and Christ, there's no question I'd pick Christ, but the Bible doesn't teach that you must choose between them, only that you must choose their priority in your life. If you put God first, all the other things will be added unto you. The secret to not losing your soul in the process of gaining the world is to make sure your priority is the Kingdom of God. You must choose to forsake everything for the Gospel. When you do, it prevents problems. A self-entitled mentality leads to crisis and destruction, but when you prioritize God and His Kingdom, you'll never lose your soul in the process.

When I was young, "things" mattered, but as the years have gone by, we have more money in the bank than ever before, and all those material things seem insignificant to me. I used to want designer clothes and jewelry. Now, I shop at Walmart because things don't have a hold on me—they're not my priority. My priority is making an impact for the Kingdom of God. When you turn away from self-indulgence and greed, you stop caring about what people think. That's how you find life and gain purpose and God begins to bless you.

An old Baptist preacher used to say, "It's hard to fall away from something you're pushing." It's one thing to be a Christian, but if you're also furthering the Gospel and soul-winning, it's difficult to fall away.

You must get certain things settled in your mind before becoming an uncommon achiever. The time to decide your principles is when you first begin. Otherwise, you'll be driven by what you've built instead of by your spirit.

Backsliding is never a blowout; it's always a slow, steady leak. That's why you must proactively prioritize things in your life, like attending church on Sunday. You need to set standards and refuse to break them. There are things I won't do, places I won't go, and actions I won't take because I have standards. If you don't settle those upfront, it's easy for the ends to justify the means. Your life will be ruled by the tyranny of the seemingly urgent, and you'll always be conflicted.

What does it profit if a man gains the whole world and loses his soul? That's a serious question. America teaches the opposite. It teaches you how to sell your soul to gain the whole world. The Lord had Jesse Duplantis walk away from a highly successful rock and roll career that began when he was just fourteen years old. He had always wanted to be successful in the music industry, but the Lord wanted Jesse to serve Him instead. He was already successful and wealthy when the Lord told him to walk away from it all and preach. Today, he has more than any rock star I've ever heard. When you put the Lord first, it's not at the expense of taking the world—it's so the world doesn't take you in the process.

AFTERWORD

I pray that God would keep a grace on you to maintain dominion over your flesh and the things of this world as you continue to pursue your dream. I thank God for enabling you to guard your heart against what this world offers.

I pray the Holy Spirit would come alive on the inside of you and that whenever the temptation to prioritize things outside of God's Word arises, His Spirit would come alive and give you a Holy Ghost kick in the head. Whenever anything attempts to distract you from God and His Kingdom, may you be reminded of Mark 8:35: *"Whoever wants to save his life has to lose it but whoever loses his life for my sake and for the sake of the gospel will save it."*

Let that be your heart's cry today. Let everything you do be unto God and for His Kingdom's sake. As you continue to prioritize God's Kingdom, it will keep you in line with His plan for your life. You won't have to take a step to the left or the right. When you keep Him first, He will add all these things unto you: joy, peace, prosperity, homes, vehicles, and the blessing.

Don't just be a hearer or reader of the Word—adhere to the instructions contained in His Word and put them into practice. The Bible says, *"Those who accept my commandments and obey them are the ones who love me"* (John 14:21). As you've read and received instruction from the Word of God, choose to walk in obedience to your Father in everything you do, in Jesus' name, Amen.

STARTING YOUR JOURNEY

Your journey to the top begins with surrendering your heart to Jesus and making Him the Lord of your life. If you can't look back to a point in time when you took this vital step, why not take care of it right now and get started on the most exciting journey available to humankind?

Jesus is alive, and through a great mystery, He will come to live in your heart. Don't come this close and reject Him. No one, having read this book, should go to Hell. You must give Jesus your life through an act of your will. He will not come and take it, it's yours to give—or not. He stands at the door and knocks, but it's up to you to open the door to your heart. You must have the courage to step out of the muck and mire of sin, receive Christ as Savior, and live a righteous life.

You can start your journey from wherever you are at this

moment and tell the Devil goodbye! Start by praying this prayer out loud:

Heavenly Father, I turn my back on sin. I believe in my heart that You raised Jesus from the dead. I confess Jesus as my Lord and Savior. Come live in my heart, fill me with Your power; make me strong where I am weak. In Jesus' name, I am saved, I am forgiven, Heaven is my home, I'll never turn back. I pray in Jesus' name, amen!

If you prayed the above prayer, you are a joint heir to the Kingdom of God, Jesus is your brother, and you have a whole new family. Your sins are forgiven! Start by telling someone.

Let us help you with the next steps so you can get your journey started right. Contact us by calling the phone number listed at the bottom of this page. We have a free gift for you. All you need to do is ask. You can call or email us to communicate with some great people who love you, care about your success, and want to pray with and for you. Reach out to us as your next step.

Congratulations on making the best decision of your life, and welcome to the start of an amazing journey—take your place at the top!

Welcome to the family of God!

Call: 412-787-2578

NOTES

2. SECRET 2

i. https://www.inc.com/marla-tabaka/this-study-found-1-simple-step-to-practically-guarantee-youll-achieve-your-goals-for-real.html#

JONATHAN AND ADALIS SHUTTLESWORTH

Evangelists Jonathan and Adalis Shuttlesworth have been preaching the Gospel full-time since May 2002. Revival Today, founded in 2007, is a ministry dedicated to reaching those who have never heard the Gospel of Jesus Christ. Over the past 20 years, Jonathan has traveled extensively throughout North America, India, the Caribbean, and Central and South Africa. In 2013, Revival Today TV was launched on mainstream television. In recent years, Revival Today's online presence has expanded significantly through platforms like Facebook and YouTube.

Since 2015, Evangelist Jonathan has conducted numerous open-air crusades and outreaches in America's inner cities, dedicated to winning the lost. Revival Today's heartbeat is for souls. The nations of the world are overripe for revival, and we are determined to be a great part of it! Revival Today provides Biblical teaching on faith, healing, prosperity, freedom from sin, and living a victorious life.

Amidst the coronavirus pandemic in 2020, Check the News—a daily program covering breaking news through the lens of Biblical truth—was launched. That same year, the Revival Today app, a 24-hour streaming platform with on-demand content, also went live.

In early 2021, Evangelists Jonathan and Adalis made a historic announcement: the launch of Revival Today Church in Pittsburgh, Pennsylvania—a church that honors the Holy Spirit, wins souls, boldly proclaims the Word of God without apology, and stands as a blessing to families and the nation. Revival Today Church sparked a movement. Soon after, Revival Today Church Fort Worth opened its doors in October 2023, igniting a fire that would soon spread across America. In March 2025, Revival Today Church Los Angeles launched, followed just weeks later by Revival Today Church Arizona on Easter Sunday 2025. Today, with all four locations thriving, growing, and impacting their cities, the vision is alive, and the mandate is being fulfilled: to see this generation shaken by the power of God.

Pastors Jonathan and Adalis believe that anyone who feels the call of God to preach the Gospel must have a solid biblical foundation. It's a non-negotiable—but it is not enough. Strong Biblical training, combined with the power of the Holy Ghost, is essential for raising up the next generation of the world.

God has called Revival Today to establish Revival Today Bible Institute—a training school designed to equip this generation to answer His call. The mission of RTBI is clear: to raise up ministers of excellence who will deliver the Gospel of Jesus Christ with both Word and Power.

If you need help or would like to partner with Revival Today to see this generation and nation transformed through The Gospel, follow these links…

www.RevivalToday.com
www.RevivalTodayChurch.com

Get access to our 24/7 network Revival Today Global Broadcast. Download the Revival Today app in your Apple App Store or Google Play Store. Watch live on Apple TV, Roku, Amazon Fire TV, and Android TV.

Call: 412-787-2578

facebook.com/revivaltoday
x.com/jdshuttlesworth
instagram.com/jdshuttlesworth
youtube.com/@jonathanshuttlesworth

DO SOMETHING TODAY THAT WILL CHANGE YOUR LIFE FOREVER

Thus saith the Lord, **make this valley full of ditches.** For thus saith the Lord, ye shall not see wind, neither shall ye see rain; Yet that valley shall be filled with water... **This is but a light thing in the sight of the Lord**... And it came to pass... **the country was filled with water.**

2 Kings 3:16-18; 20

Revival is the only answer to the problems of this country - nothing more, nothing less, nothing else.

Thank you for standing with me as a partner with Revival Today. We must see this nation shaken by the power of God.

You cannot ask God to bless you first, prior to giving. God asks you to step out first in your giving - and then He makes it rain. We are believing God for 1,000 people to partner with us monthly at $84. Something everyone can do, but a significant seed that will connect you to the rainmaker.

IF YOU HAVE NOT YET PARTNERED WITH REVIVAL TODAY, JOIN US TODAY!

This year is not your year to dig small ditches. When I grew tired of small meetings and altar calls, I moved forward in faith and God responded. God is the rainmaker, but you must give Him something to fill. It's time for you to move forward! **Will you stand with me today to see the nations of the world shaken by the power of God?**

Revivaltoday.com/give

revivaltoday.com/paypal

Zelle® info@revivaltoday.com

venmo @RTgive

Text "GIVE" to 75767
Call at (412) 787-2578

Mail a check to:

Revival Today P.O. BOX 7
PROSPERITY PA 15329

REVIVAL TODAY
Email: info@revivaltoday.com

www.ingramcontent.com/pod-product-compliance
Lightning Source LLC
Chambersburg PA
CBHW040252170426
43191CB00019B/2390